Math in Focus®
Singapore Math
by Marshall Cavendish

Transition Guide

For New Program Implementation
and Intervention

Marshall Cavendish
Education

US Distributor

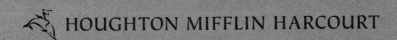
HOUGHTON MIFFLIN HARCOURT

COMMON
CORE

© 2012 Marshall Cavendish International (Singapore) Private Limited

Published by Marshall Cavendish Education
An imprint of Marshall Cavendish International (Singapore) Private Limited
Times Centre, 1 New Industrial Road, Singapore 536196
Customer Service Hotline: (65) 6411 0820
E-mail: tmesales@sg.marshallcavendish.com
Website: www.marshallcavendish.com/education

Common Core Standards © Copyright 2010.
National Governors Association Center for Best Practices and
Council of Chief State School Officers. All rights reserved.

This product is not sponsored or endorsed by the Common Core State Standards
Initiative of the National Governors Association Center for Best Practices and
the Council of Chief State School Officers.

Distributed by
Houghton Mifflin Harcourt
222 Berkeley Street
Boston, MA 02116
Tel: 617-351-5000
Website: www.hmheducation.com/mathinfocus

First published 2012

Marshall Cavendish and *Math in Focus®* are trademarks of Times
Publishing Limited.

Math in Focus® Transition Guide Course 1
ISBN 978-0-547-57909-2

Printed in United States of America

2 3 4 5 6 7 8 1409   17 16 15 14 13 12 11
4500310751   A B C D E

Math in Focus

Singapore Math
by Marshall Cavendish

Introduction

The *Math in Focus Transition Guide* provides a map to help transition teachers and students new to the Math in Focus program.

Much of the success of Singapore math is due to the careful way in which algorithms are developed, with an emphasis on understanding. Lessons move from concrete models to pictorial and symbolic representations. Students develop mathematical ideas in depth, and see how the concepts are connected and that mathematics is not a series of isolated skills.

Teaching to Mastery With Student Proficiency

Singapore has been scoring at the top of international comparison studies for over 15 years. One of the key characteristics of the Singapore curriculum is teaching to mastery. This Transition Guide is designed to help teachers as they transition their students into *Math in Focus*.

What Does Transition Mean?

Transitioning in *Math in Focus* is the process of using specific methods to teach concepts and skills students have not yet mastered or been exposed to at previous grade levels, so they can attain mastery at their current grade level.

What is the Difference Between Transition and Intervention?

Transition is providing students with the needed exposure to topics and methods that were taught in the previous grade levels. Intervention is serving students who have had repeated exposure and lack mastery. The transition process is beneficial to students who require intervention.

Using the Transition Guide

- *The Transition Guide* Math Background addresses five critical strands: Number Sense (NS), Ratios and Proportional Relationships (RP), Expressions and Equations (EE), Geometry (G), and Statistics and Probability (SP). Additional Math Background support is provided at the beginning of each chapter in the *Math in Focus* Teacher's Guide.

- The *Math Background* topics were chosen to help teachers understand and apply the Singapore approach upon which *Math in Focus* is based. These topics are either introduced earlier than in other programs or are presented differently in this program.

- The classroom teacher can easily scan through the *Math Background* to determine the set of skills and concepts taught in prior years. Ensuring that a student has these background skills will help the student succeed in this program.

- For each skill objective, there are *Transition Worksheets*. These worksheets provide step-by-step instruction, practice, and review. A student can follow the steps independently or with someone's help. Corresponding teacher guides provide alternate teaching strategies, checks, and intervention suggestions.

  The *Transition Guide* is also available Online and on the Teacher One-Stop CD-ROM.

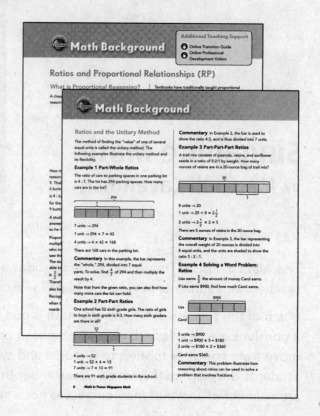

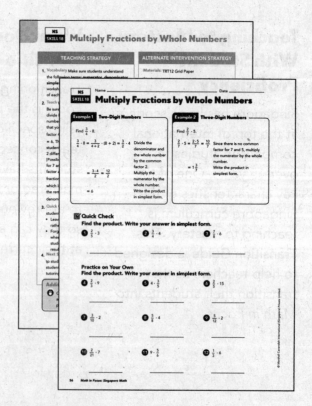

How does a teacher transition students? It's as easy as 1-2-3-4!

①

Administer diagnostic test.

Use the items on the Chapter Pre-Test in *Assessments* book to determine whether a student has the necessary prerequisite skills for success in this chapter.

②

Examine the diagnostic test for each student's strengths and weaknesses.

Use Recall Prior Knowledge and Quick Check in the *Student Edition* to review concepts and check for understanding.

③

Determine the instructional pathway for each student.

Use the Resource Planner in the *Transition Guide* to find the appropriate Math Background and Skills worksheets.

④

Intervene, reinforce, and assess.

Use online *Reteach* and *Extra Practice* worksheets from one- or two-grades below.

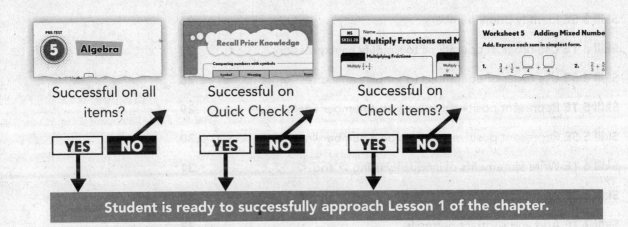

Successful on all items?

Successful on Quick Check?

Successful on Check items?

| YES | NO | | YES | NO | | YES | NO |

Student is ready to successfully approach Lesson 1 of the chapter.

Flexible Approach

Depending on your needs, you can also use the Recall Prior Knowledge Quick Check questions in the *Student Edition* to determine whether your students have the prerequisite skills for a chapter. The Chapter Pre-Test in the *Assessments* book can then serve as a check for understanding. You can also bypass Step 1 or Step 2.

Course 1 Contents

Course 1 Resource Planner

TRANSITION SKILLS AND RESOURCES

STRAND/ SKILL	SKILL OBJECTIVE	ASSESSMENTS PRE-TEST	STUDENT BOOK
NS 1	Find factors of a whole number.	Chapter 1: Items 1–2	Ch 1 RPK, QC 1–4
NS 2	Find multiples of a whole number.	Chapter 1: Items 3–4	Ch 1 RPK, QC 5–8
NS 3	Identify prime numbers.	Chapter 1: Items 5–6	Ch 1 RPK, QC 9
NS 4	Use order of operations to simplify an expression.	Chapter 1: Items 7–8	Ch 1 RPK, QC 10–11
NS 5	Representing positive numbers on a number line.	Chapter 2: Items 1–3	Ch 2 RPK, QC 1–3
NS 6	Writing statements of inequality using $>$ and $<$.	Chapter 2: Items 4–7	Ch 2 RPK, QC 4–6
NS 7	Add and subtract decimals.	Chapter 3: Items 1–2	Ch 3 RPK, QC 1–4
NS 8	Express improper fractions as mixed numbers.	Chapter 3: Items 3–4	Ch 3 RPK, QC 5–10
NS 9	Express mixed numbers as improper fractions.	Chapter 3: Items 5–6	Ch 3 RPK, QC 11–13
NS 10	Multiply fractions by fractions.	Chapter 3: Items 7–8 Chapter 5: Items 5–6	Ch 3 RPK, QC 14–16 Ch 5 RPK, QC 9–10
NS 11	Write equivalent fractions by multiplication.	Chapter 4: Items 1–2	Ch 4 RPK, QC 1–3
NS 12	Write equivalent fractions by division.	Chapter 4: Items 3–4	Ch 4 RPK, QC 4–6
NS 13	Complete equivalent fractions.	Chapter 4: Items 5–8	Ch 4 RPK, QC 7–10
NS 14	Write fractions in simplest form.	Chapter 4: Items 9–10	Ch 4 RPK, QC 11–13
NS 15	Convert measurements.	Chapter 4: Items 11–12	Ch 4 RPK, QC 14–19
NS 16	Interpret a comparison bar model.	Chapter 4: Items 13–14	Ch 4 RPK, QC 20–21
NS 17	Multiply whole numbers.	Chapter 5: Items 1–2	Ch 5 RPK, QC 1–4
NS 18	Multiply fractions by a whole number.	Chapter 5: Item 3	Ch 5 RPK, QC 5–6
NS 19	Multiply mixed numbers and whole numbers.	Chapter 5: Item 4	Ch 5 RPK, QC 7–8
NS 20	Divide with fractions and whole numbers.	Chapter 5: Items 7–8	Ch 5 RPK, QC 11–14
NS 21	Divide fractions.	Chapter 5: Items 9–10	Ch 5 RPK, QC 15–16
NS 22	Find the quantity represented by a number of units.	Chapter 5: Items 11–12	Ch 5 RPK, QC 17–18
RP 23	Find ratios.	Chapter 5: Items 3–16	Ch 5 RPK, QC 19–24
NS 24	Find equivalent fractions using multiplication.	Chapter 6: Items 1–4	Ch 5 RPK, QC 1–2
NS 25	Simplify fractions using division.	Chapter 6: Items 5–6	Ch 6: Items 3–4
NS 26	Write fractions with a denominator of 100 as decimals.	Chapter 6: Items 7–8	Ch 6: Items 5–10

KEY: RPK (Recall Prior Knowledge), QC (Quick Check)

GRADE 5 RETEACH	GRADE 5 EXTRA PRACTICE	GRADE 4 RETEACH	GRADE 4 EXTRA PRACTICE
		4A pp. 23–31	4A Lesson 2.2
		4A pp. 33–38	4A Lesson 2.3
		4A pp. 31–32	4A Lesson 2.2
5A pp. 31–32	5A Lesson 2.6		
5A pp. 9–15; 5B pp. 9–16	5A Lesson 1.4; 5B Lesson 8.2	4A pp. 9–12; 4B pp. 29–46	4A Lesson 1.2; 4B Lesson 7.3
		4B pp. 57–94	4B Lesson 8.1–8.3
		4A pp. 165–172	4A Lesson 6.5
		4A pp. 159–172	4A Lessons 6.4–6.5
5A pp. 117–130	5A Lesson 4.1, 4.3		
		4A pp. 71–76	4A Lesson 3.5
5A pp. 31–46	5A Lessons 2.2–2.3	4A pp. 39–58	4A Lesson 3.1–3.2
		4A pp. 181–186	4A Lesson 6.7
5A pp. 131–132	5A Lesson 4.4		
5A pp. 137–140	5A Lesson 4.6		
5A pp. 186–198	5A Lesson 7.4, 7.7		
5A, pp. 171–180	5A Lessons 7.1–7.2		
		4B, pp. 51–56	4B Lesson 7.5

Course 1 Resource Planner

TRANSITION SKILLS AND RESOURCES

STRAND/ SKILL	SKILL OBJECTIVE	ASSESSMENTS PRE-TEST	STUDENT BOOK
NS 27	Multiply fractions by whole numbers.	Chapter 6: Items 9–10	Ch 6: RPK, QC 11–16
NS 28	Use bar models to show the four operations.	Chapter 7: Items 1–4	Ch 7: RPK, QC 1–4
NS 29	Find common factors and greatest common factors.	Chapter 7: Items 5–7	Ch 7: RPK, QC 5–8
NS 30	Understand mathermatical terms.	Chapter 7: Items 8–11	Ch 7: RPK, QC 9–12
NS 31	Compare numbers using > and <.	Chapter 8: Items 1–8	Ch 8: RPK, QC 1–4
EE 32	Use variables to write algebraic expressions.	Chapter 8: Items 9–14	Ch 8: RPK, QC 5–8
NS 33	Evaluate algebraic expressions.	Chapter 8: Items 15–18	Ch 8: RPK, QC 9–10
NS 34	Plot points on a coordinate plane.	Chapter 8: Items 19–20	Ch 8: RPK, QC 11
NS 35	Identify and plot coordinates.	Chapter 9: Items 1–2	Ch 9: RPK, QC 1–2
NS 36	Represent negative numbers on the number line.	Chapter 9: Items 3	Ch 9: RPK, QC 3–5
NS 37	Identify the absolute value of a number.	Chapter 9: Items 4–7	Ch 9: RPK, QC 6–8
G 38	Find the perimeter of a polygon.	Chapter 9: Items 8–12	Ch 9: RPK, QC 9–13
G 39	Find the area of a rectangle using a formula.	Chapter 10: Items 1	Ch 10: RPK, QC 1
G 40	Find the area of a square using a formula.	Chapter 10: Items 2	Ch 10: RPK, QC 2
G 41	Identify parallelograms, trapezoids, and rhombuses.	Chapter 10: Items 3–5	Ch 10: RPK, QC 3–5
NS 42	Add decimals.	Chapter 11: Items 1–3	Ch 11: RPK, QC 1–3
NS 43	Subtract decimals.	Chapter 11: Items 4–6	Ch 11: RPK, QC 4–6
NS 44	Multiply decimals.	Chapter 11: Items 7–9	Ch 11: RPK, QC 7–9
NS 45	Divide decimals.	Chapter 11: Items 10–12	Ch 11: RPK, QC 10–15
NS 46	Round numbers to the nearest whole number.	Chapter 11: Items 13–15	Ch 11: RPK, QC 16–21
NS 47	Round numbers to the nearest tenth.	Chapter 11: Items 16–18	Ch 11: RPK, QC 22–30
G 48	Identify special prisms.	Chapter 12: Items 1	Ch 12: RPK, QC 1–3
G 49	Find areas of rectangles, triangles, and trapezoids.	Chapter 12: Items 2–4	Ch 12: RPK, QC 4–7
G 50	Find volumes of cubes and rectangular prisms.	Chapter 12: Items 5–6	Ch 12: RPK, QC 8–11
SP 51	Interpret data in a line plot.	Chapter 13: Items 1–8	Ch 13: RPK, QC 1–10
NS 52	Divide decimals by a whole number.	Chapter 14: Items 1–4	Ch 14: RPK, QC 1–2
SP 53	Find the average of a data set.	Chapter 14: Items 5–7	Ch 14: RPK, QC 3–6

KEY: RPK (Recall Prior Knowledge), QC (Quick Check)

GRADE 5 RETEACH	GRADE 5 EXTRA PRACTICE	GRADE 4 RETEACH	GRADE 4 EXTRA PRACTICE
5A pp. 141–142	5A Lesson 4.7	4A pp. 181–186	4A Lesson 6.7
		4A, pp. 27–31	Lesson 2.2
5A pp. 143–146	5A Lesson 5.1		
5A pp. 147–152	5A Lesson 5.2		
		4A pp. 91–94	4A Lesson 4.3
5B pp. 103–106	5B Lesson 11.2		
		4B pp. 121–128	4B Lesson 12.1
		4B pp. 135–138	4B Lesson 12.2
5B pp. 147–152	5B Lesson 13.5		
		4B pp. 57–74	4B Lesson 8.1
		4B, pp. 75–90	4B Lesson 8.5
5B pp. 19–30	5B Lesson 9.1		
5B pp. 39–53	5B Lesson 9.3		
		4B pp. 47–48	4B Lesson 7.4
		4B pp. 49–50	4B Lesson 7.4
5B pp. 153–158	5B Lesson 14.1		
5A pp. 159–167	5A Lesson 6.1–6.2		
5B pp. 259–295	5B Lesson 15.1–15.5		
		4A pp. 95–100	4A Lesson 5.1

KEY: RPK (Recall Prior Knowledge), QC (Quick Check)

Math Background

Additional Teaching Support
- Online Transition Guide
- Online Professional Development Videos

The Number System (NS)

A Variety of Methods for Representing Numbers

Students using the Singapore approach to mathematics become familiar with multiple ways to represent numbers beginning in the primary grades. From their very earliest experiences with whole-number place value, students learn to use place-value chips to show the powers of ten that are the basis of our number system. Here, for example, a student uses place-value chips and a place-value chart to model the number 653,104.

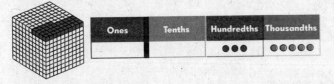

When students broaden their understanding of "number" beyond whole numbers to include fractions in decimal form, previously-learned and familiar models continue to play a crucial role in concept building.

Place-value chips are often juxtaposed with base-ten models to help students interpret numbers in different ways. Here are two different representations for the decimal 0.35.

The set of rational numbers includes fractions as well as decimals. But place-value charts are not particularly useful for fraction models. Instead, grid models are combined with number lines to show how fractions and decimals are related. This model helps students relate $\frac{45}{100}$ to 0.45.

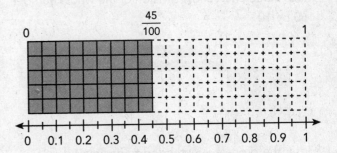

The multiple representations for numbers in Singapore math go far beyond developing basic number sense. The same models are used to help students learn how—and why—computational algorithms work. An example of whole-number division from earlier grades illustrates how students can use place-value chips to model the regrouping that is part of almost all number computation.

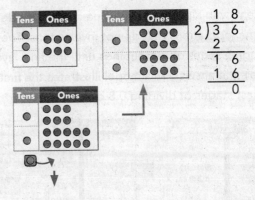

Regrouping is also involved in understanding place value with decimals. Here, students use place-value chips and a place-value chart to show why 12 thousandths is written in the decimal form 0.012.

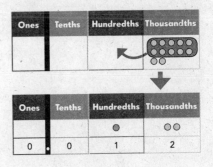

The same manipulatives can be used to model operations. Below, place-value chips and a place-value chart show division of the whole number 160 by 10.

	Thousands	Hundreds	Tens	Ones
160		●	●●●●●	
160 ÷ 10			●●	●●●●●●

Here, the process is extended to decimals. Multiplying and dividing by powers of 10 plays a key role in the development of decimal concepts.

	Hundreds	Tens	Ones	Tenths	Hundredths	Thousandths
16.8		1	6	8		
16.8 × 10	1	6	8			
1.68			1	6	8	
1.68 × 10		1	6	8		
1.608			1	6	0	8
1.608 × 10		1	6	0	8	

Students can also use place-value chips to model decimal operations that do not involve tens. They go through a series of regroupings until the final layout reveals the answer. This model illustrates the first and last stages of dividing 0.8 by 5.

Ones	Tenths
	●●●●
	●●●●

→

Ones	Tenths	Hundredths
	●	●●●●●
	●	●●●●●
	●	●●●●●
	●	●●●●●
	●	●●●●●

Students who have studied Singapore math have used bar modeling and the unitary method to solve whole-number word problems. The same models can be used to solve problems involving fractions and decimals, as below.

A piece of metal is 6.54 yards long. It is cut into two pieces. One piece is twice as long as the other. What is the length of the longer piece?

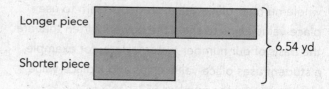

From the model, 3 units = 6.54 yd.

3 units → 6.54

1 unit → 6.54 ÷ 3 = 2.18

2 units → 2.18 · 2 = 4.36

The longer piece is 4.36 yards long.

From number meanings to operations to problem solving, the Singapore use of models gives students powerful visualizing tools. The bar modeling and unitary method that work so well with whole numbers are equally effective in problem-solving applications involving fractions and decimals.

Number Line Models for Equivalence and Integers

Number line models emphasize the connections between fractions and decimals and help to lay the groundwork for an eventual understanding of the set of real numbers.

Example 1 Comparing Numbers in Different Forms

Which is greater, $\frac{3}{5}$ or 0.7?

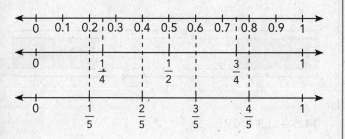

$\frac{3}{5} = 0.6$

0.6 lies to the left of 0.7.

So, $\frac{3}{5} < 0.7$.

Example 2 Representing Integers

Draw a vertical number line to represent the following set of numbers.

−13, −10, −15, −11

Choose a number less than the least number in the set. The least number is −15, so start with −16.

Draw the number line from the bottom up until you have included all four numbers. Add one more integer at the top.

$$
\begin{array}{l}
-10 \bullet \\
-11 \bullet \\
-12 \\
-13 \bullet \\
-14 \\
-15 \bullet \\
-16
\end{array}
$$

Fraction and Decimal Multiplication and Division

By the end of Grade 5, students have mastered all four operations with whole numbers, as well as addition and subtraction of fractions and decimals. This course concludes that work by introducing multiplication and division with both fractions and decimals. Course 2 will introduce use of the four operations with integers.

Example 3 Dividing by a Fraction

Betty used $\frac{2}{3}$ jar of poster paint to paint one election poster. How many posters can she complete with 5 jars of paint?

To solve the problem, divide 5 by $\frac{2}{3}$. First divide each of 5 whole bars into 3 equal parts. Then shade the parts in groups of $\frac{2}{3}$.

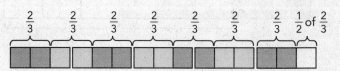

Number of two-thirds in 2 wholes = 3

Number of two-thirds in 1 whole = $1\frac{1}{2}$ or $\frac{3}{2}$

Number of two-thirds in 5 wholes = $5 \cdot \frac{3}{2}$

So, $5 \div \frac{2}{3} = 5 \cdot \frac{3}{2}$

$$= \frac{15}{2}$$

$$= 7\frac{1}{2}$$

Betty can paint $7\frac{1}{2}$ posters with 5 jars of paint.

Bar Modeling with Fractions and Decimals

Because educators in the United States may be unfamiliar with the unitary method and bar modeling, these final two examples illustrate the power of these visualization strategies.

Example 4 Unitary Models with Fractions

Derrick's school has a chess and checkers club. $\frac{1}{4}$ of the members play in chess tournaments.

The rest compete in checkers. One-half of the checkers players are girls. The club has 72 members in all. How many checkers players are boys?

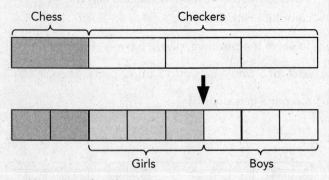

Students begin by drawing a bar divided into equal fourths to show the fractions of the club that play chess and checkers.

3 of the 4 parts of the bar show checker players. Because half of the checkers players are girls, those 3 bars must be divided into 2 equal parts. To do that, students must divide the 3 equal parts into 6 equal parts. So, the whole bar must be divided into 8 equal parts.

The model shows that $\frac{3}{8}$ of the members of the club who play checkers are boys. The whole bar represents the 72 members in the club.

8 units → 72
 1 unit → 72 ÷ 8 = 9
3 units → 3 · 9 = 27

There are 27 boys in the club who play checkers.

Commentary The method of finding the value of one of several equal units is called the unitary method. In this example, students use the method to solve a complex problem involving fractions. They will also find this approach effective in problems that involve ratio, proportion, and percent.

Example 5 Modeling Decimal Division

Gayle and her brother made 14.5 L of tomato salsa. They are filling gift jars that each hold 0.5 L. How many jars can they fill?

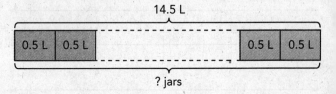

14.5 ÷ 0.5 = 29

Gayle and her brother can fill 29 jars with tomato salsa.

Commentary This particular division model may be new to most teachers and students. The dashed lines at the center of the bar indicate that the quantity of equal parts the whole bar is divided into is unknown. Because the model works equally well with decimals and fractions as with whole numbers, students can make use of it for any type of division situation.

> ### Additional Teaching Resource
>
> For additional reading, see *The Singapore Model Method for Learning Mathematics* published by the Ministry of Education of Singapore and *Bar Modeling: A Problem-solving Tool* by Yeap Ban Har, published by Marshall Cavendish Education.

Math Background

Ratios and Proportional Relationships (RP)

What is Proportional Reasoning?

A classic test for acquisition of proportional reasoning is the Short Man-Tall Man problem.

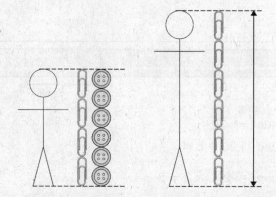

How many buttons tall is the tall man? Students who reason proportionally arrive at the correct answer of 9. That is, the short man is 4 paperclips tall and 6 buttons tall, and the ratio of paperclips to buttons is 4 : 6, or $\frac{3}{4}$. If the ratio of paperclips to buttons for the tall man is the same, then the tall man is 9 buttons tall.

A student, at an earlier stage of development, may answer 8, reasoning that Mr. Tall is 2 paperclips taller, so he must be 2 buttons taller also.

Proportional thinking requires students to use multiplicative, not additive reasoning. The student who incorrectly gave 8 as the height of the tall man saw the increase in height as an additive increase. The student who gave the correct height of 9 was able to see that the tall man's "paperclip height" is $\frac{3}{2}$ the "paperclip height" of the short man. Therefore the "button height" of the tall man must also be $\frac{3}{2}$ the "button height" of the short man Recognizing a multiplicative relationship, especially when the ratio is a fraction, such as $\frac{3}{2}$, is a task that needs much development.

Textbooks have traditionally taught proportional reasoning by using pictures of discrete objects to illustrate equivalent ratios, as shown below. Textbooks may then move on to using cross products of equal ratios to solve proportional reasoning problems.

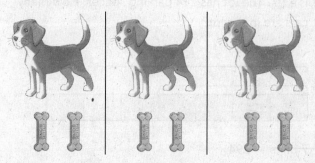

Ratios: 1 dog : 2 bones
2 dogs : 4 bones
3 dogs : 6 bones

Proportion: $\frac{2}{4} = \frac{3}{6} \rightarrow 2 \times 6 = 4 \times 4$

A potential weakness of this approach is that students may learn to solve proportions without truly understanding how to apply proportional reasoning in problem contexts.

The Singapore approach emphasizes modeling and the unitary method to achieve a broader understanding of proportionality. Because the bar model is a continuous rather than a discrete model, it is more robust, fitting more contexts than discrete models, and allowing students to analyze and solve complex proportion problems.

Because educators in the United States may be unfamiliar with bar models and the unitary method, the next few pages are devoted to examining these two important problem-solving strategies. Examples are provided; as these examples increase in complexity, so too do the models.

Ratios and the Unitary Method

The method of finding the "value" of one of several equal units is called the unitary method. The following examples illustrate the unitary method and its flexibility.

Example 1 Part-Whole Ratios

The ratio of cars to parking spaces in one parking lot is 4 : 7. The lot has 294 parking spaces. How many cars are in the lot?

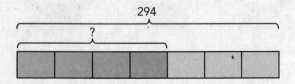

7 units → 294

1 unit → 294 ÷ 7 = 42

4 units → 4 × 42 = 168

There are 168 cars in the parking lot.

Commentary In this example, the bar represents the "whole," 294, divided into 7 equal parts. To solve, find $\frac{4}{7}$ of 294 and then multiply the result by 4.

Note that from the given ratio, you can also find how many more cars the lot can hold.

Example 2 Part-Part Ratios

One school has 52 sixth grade girls. The ratio of girls to boys in sixth grade is 4:3. How many sixth graders are there in all?

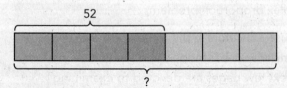

4 units → 52
1 unit → 52 ÷ 4 = 13
7 units → 7 × 13 = 91

There are 91 sixth grade students in the school.

Commentary In Example 2, the bar is used to show the ratio 4:3, and is thus divided into 7 units.

Example 3 Part-Part-Part Ratios

A trail mix consists of peanuts, raisins, and sunflower seeds in a ratio of 5:2:1 by weight. How many ounces of raisins are in a 20-ounce bag of trail mix?

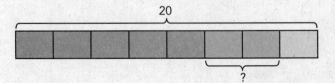

8 units → 20

1 unit → 20 ÷ 8 = $2\frac{1}{2}$

2 units → $2\frac{1}{2}$ × 2 = 5

There are 5 ounces of raisins in the 20-ounce bag.

Commentary In Example 3, the bar representing the overall weight of 20 ounces is divided into 8 equal units, and the units are shaded to show the ratio 5 : 2 : 1.

Example 4 Solving a Word Problem: Ratios

Lisa earns $\frac{5}{2}$ the amount of money Carol earns. If Lisa earns $900, find how much Carol earns.

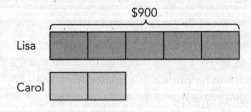

5 units → $900
1 unit → $900 × 5 = $180
2 units → $180 × 2 = $360

Carol earns $360.

Commentary This problem illustrates how reasoning about ratios can be used to solve a problem that involves fractions.

Rates, a Context for Ratios

Rates are ratios that compare two measures with unlike units. Some familiar rates are speed (miles per hour), gasoline consumption (miles per gallon), and unit cost (dollars per unit). The following three examples apply bar models and/or the unitary method to various types of rate problems.

Example 5 Calculating a Unit Rate

Mr. Lester drove 270 miles and used 12.5 gallons of gas. What kind of gas mileage does his car get?

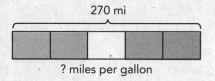

270 mi

? miles per gallon

12.5 units → 270
1 unit → 270 ÷ 12.5 = 21.6

The car gets 21.6 miles per gallon.

Example 6 Solving a Word Problem: Rates

At a farm stand, a dozen ears of sweet corn sell for $5. How much do 8 ears cost?

12 units → 5

1 unit → 5 ÷ 12 = $\frac{5}{12}$

8 units → 8 × $\frac{5}{12}$ = $\frac{40}{12}$ ≈ 3.34

The cost of 8 ears is $3.34.

Commentary Note that in Example 6, the cost per ear ($\frac{5}{12}$ of a dollar) is calculated, and then used to find the cost of 8 ears.

Example 7 Solving a More Complex Rate Problem

One state had a population density of 104 people per square mile in the last census. It is projected that the population will increase by 9 million by the next census. Then the population density will be 128 people per square mile. What was the state's population in the last census?

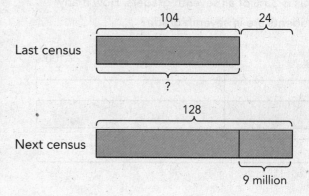

24 units → 9 million
1 unit → 9 million ÷ 24 = 0.375 million
104 units → 104 × 0.375 = 39 million

The state's population in the last census was 39 million.

Commentary At first glance, the word problem in Example 7 may not seem to include enough information. The bar model shows that indeed enough information is provided. The two bars represent the population density data from the two censuses. The labels above each bar show population density data. The labels beneath each bar show the number of people this represents.

Note that the label 24 needs to be calculated to complete the model. It is the difference in the two population densities. Note also the importance of labeling each bar when the model has more than one bar. Using labels keeps the pieces of data properly linked.

Percent Problems

The percent problems students encounter in middle school are more complex than those they have seen earlier. Using bar models helps them visualize different types of percent problems.

Example 8 Finding the Whole

The school band has 155 seventh grade students. This is 35% of all seventh graders. How many students are in seventh grade?

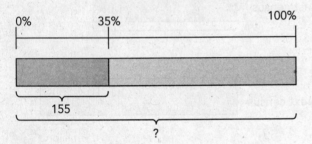

$35\% \rightarrow 155$
$1\% \rightarrow 155 \div 35 = 4.3$
$100\% \rightarrow 4.3 \times 100 = 430$

The school has 430 seventh grade students.

Example 9 Finding a Percent of Increase

A store sold 15% more peaches in July than in June. This increase amounted to 75 more pounds of peaches. How many pounds of peaches were sold in June and July?

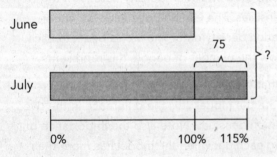

$15\% \rightarrow 75$
$1\% \rightarrow 75 \div 15 = 5$
$215\% \rightarrow 5 \times 215 = 1,075$

1,075 pounds were sold in the two months.

Example 10 Finding a Percent of Decrease

A book is divided into Parts I and II. Part I has 220 pages, and Part II has 15% fewer pages. How many pages does the whole book have?

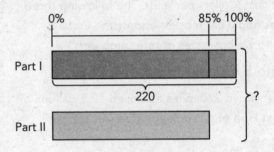

$100\% \rightarrow 220$
$1\% \rightarrow 220 \div 100 = 2.2$
$185\% \rightarrow 2.2 \times 185 = 407$

The book has 407 pages.

Commentary Two new conventions are shown on this page:

- Using a number line to divide a bar into a given ratio, and

- Using a brace to indicate the sum of the data in two or more bars.

These conventions extend the types of problems that can be visualized with bar models. Note that the bar model used for the problem in Example 10 could be used to answer other questions such as:

- How many pages does Part II have?

- How many pages more than Part II does Part I have?

Additional Teaching Resource

For additional reading, see *The Singapore Model Method for Learning Mathematics* published by the Ministry of Education of Singapore and *Bar Modeling: A Problem-solving Tool* by Yeap Ban Har, published by Marshall Cavendish Education.

Math Background

PROFESSIONAL LEARNING

Additional Teaching Support

- Online Transition Guide
- Online Professional Development Videos

Expressions and Equations (EE)

Expressions, Equations, Inequalities, and Bar Models

In secondary school, students take the arithmetic skills they have learned and begin to apply them to algebra. Often students have difficulty formulating algebraic equations to represent information given in word problems. A major strength of the Singapore approach is the ease with which algebraic structure can be superimposed on bar models to ease this transition.

In Grade 4, students learned to identify and extend numeric and nonnumeric patterns, and to use rules to describe these patterns. They wrote and solved number sentences for multi-step problems. In Grade 5, students applied their pattern skills to numeric patterns involving all operations. They extended their number-sentence skills to writing and solving equations, and they began to explore the use of letters as variables in both expressions and equations.

The following simple problem shows the connection between an algebraic solution and a solution using bar models.

Patrick weighs 16 pounds more than his brother David. Their total weight is 200 pounds. What is Patrick's weight?

The traditional algebraic method involves assigning a variable to represent an unknown quantity. Let David's weight be x pounds. Then Patrick's weight is $x + 16$ pounds.

$$\text{Total weight} = x + (x + 16)$$
$$= 2x + 16$$
$$200 = 2x + 16$$
$$184 = 2x$$
$$92 = x$$

Patrick's weight is $x + 16$ or $92 + 16 = 108$ pounds.

In Singapore, students draw a comparison bar model to represent the problem situation.

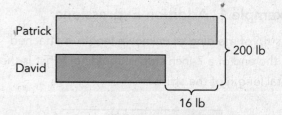

The problem can then be solved algebraically by assigning David's weight a value of x.

With revised labeling, the model can also be used to solve the problem without using variables by employing the unitary method.

Let David's weight be 1 unit.

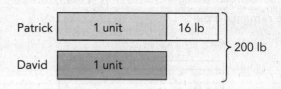

Total weight is 2 units + 16.

$$2 \text{ units} + 16 = 200$$
$$2 \text{ units} = 200 - 16 = 184$$
$$1 \text{ unit} = 184 \div 2 = 92$$

Patrick weighs $92 + 16 = 108$ pounds.

Balance-scale models, line graphs, and number line models are used both traditionally and in Singapore math to visualize and solve equations and inequalities.

For educators in the United States who may be unsure of how to use bar modeling in an algebraic context, the next few pages develop the use of bar models in algebraic situations.

Math Background

Expressions and Bar Models

Bar models can be used to represent real-world algebraic situations. In algebra, variables are used to represent unknown quantities, in place of the questions marks used in arithmetic operations.

Example 1 Addition Expressions

A strip of molding of unknown length is attached to the end of a 7-inch strip of molding. What is the total length of the strips?

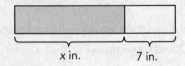

Length: $(x + 7)$ inches

Example 2 Subtraction Expressions

A piece of yarn y centimeters long is cut from a 12-centimeter piece of yarn What is the length of the remaining piece?

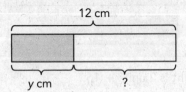

Length: $(12 - y)$ centimeters

Example 3 Multiplication Expressions

There are z sheets of paper in a small pad. How many sheets of paper are in 6 of these pads?

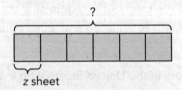

Sheets of paper: $6z$

Example 4 Division Expressions

A strip of paper is w inches long. It is divided into 4 equal parts. What is the length of each part?

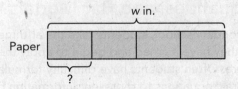

Length of each part: $w \div 4$ in. or $\frac{w}{4}$ in.

Commentary In these examples, bar modeling allows students to identify the known and unknown quantities and to visualize their relationships. It also helps them make sense of using a variable to represent an unknown quantity in a problem.

Evaluating Expressions

Once students have learned to use bar models to visualize algebraic situations and write expressions, they can evaluate the expressions for given values.

Example 5 Evaluating Subtraction Expressions

Jorge has x seashells and Kerry has 3 seashells. How many more seashells does Jorgé have than Kerry?

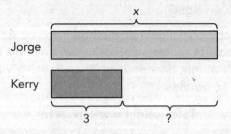

From the model, Jorge has $(x - 3)$ more seashells than Kerry.

For $x = 12$, $12 - 3 = 9$. Jorge has 9 more seashells.

For $x = 15$, $15 - 3 = 12$. Jorge has 12 more seashells.

Example 6 Evaluating Division Expressions

Kia has *m* marbles. Bill has one third as many marbles as Kia. How many marbles does Bill have?

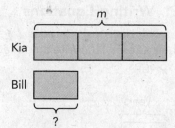

Number of marbles Bill has: $m \div 3$ or $\dfrac{m}{3}$.

For $m = 21$, $21 \div 3 = 7$. Bill has 7 marbles.

For $m = 6$, $6 \div 3 = 2$. Bill has 2 marbles.

Commentary Bar modeling is not meant to be an end in itself. Rather, as the examples show, it allows students to visualize the problem before proceeding to the more abstract algebraic representation.

Simplifying and Expanding Expressions

Bar models can also be used to help students grasp common algebraic manipulations, such as simplifying and expanding algebraic expressions.

Example 7 Simplifying Algebraic Expressions

The side of a square measures *r* inches. What is the perimeter of the square?

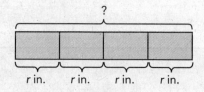

$P = r + r + r + r$

$P = 4 \cdot r = 4r$

Example 8 Expanding Algebraic Expressions

Expand $3(n + 4)$.

$3(n + 4)$ means 3 groups of $n + 4$.

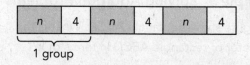

Rearrange the parts of the bar to collect like terms.

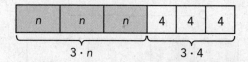

From the model, students can easily see how the expression is expanded.

$$3(n + 4) = 3 \cdot (n + 4)$$
$$= (3 \cdot n) + (3 \cdot 4)$$
$$= 3n + 12$$

Commentary Traditional algebra courses justify the steps in these two problems by calling on the properties of real numbers. In the Singapore approach, students solidify their understanding of these concepts before formalizing them. The models serve as an intuitive introduction to concepts that will be justified using the properties of real numbers in Courses 2 and 3, when the emphasis on modeling decreases. Example 8 models what students will later learn is the Distributive Property.

Solving Real-World Problems

Having learned how to write, simplify, and expand algebraic expressions, students apply those skills to solving real-world problems.

Example 9 Solving Addition Problems

The figure shows rectangle *ABCD*. What is the perimeter of rectangle *ABCD* in terms of *x*?

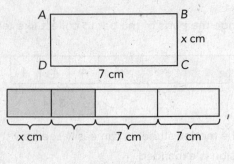

$$P = x + x + 7 + 7$$
$$= 2x + 14$$

The perimeter of rectangle *ABCD* is 2x + 14 cm.

For $x = 2$, perimeter is $2(2) + 14 = 18$ centimeters.
For $x = 5$, perimeter is $2(5) + 14 = 24$ centimeters.

Example 10 Solving Multiplication Problems

A pound of cheese costs $3. How much do *c* pounds of cheese cost?

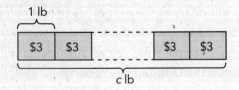

1 pound costs 3 dollars
c pounds of cheese costs 3*c* dollars

For $c = 4$, the cost is $3(4) = \$12$.
For $c = 7$, the cost is $3(7) = \$21$.

Commentary The dotted lines in the center of the bar show that the number of equal parts in the bar is unknown. This convention is used to model situations in which the size of the equal groups is known, but the number of the groups is not.

Writing Equations

Students can apply their knowledge of modeling and algebraic expressions to writing equations using one variable.

Example 11 Writing Equations

Amir is *x* years old. His cousin Jared is 7 years older. The sum of their ages is 23. Write an equation to relate their two ages.

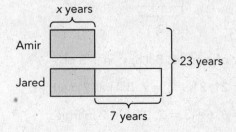

From the model, students can easily write the equation, $23 = x + (x + 7)$.

In Course 2, student will strengthen and extend the algebraic concepts mastered in Course 1. They learn to expand algebraic expressions involving decimals, to factor expressions involving negative terms, and to find solutions to equations in two variables.

Additional Teaching Resource

For additional reading, see *The Singapore Model Method for Learning Mathematics* published by the Ministry of Education of Singapore and *Bar Modeling: A Problem-solving Tool* by Yeap Ban Har, published by Marshall Cavendish Education.

Geometry (G)

Geometric Reasoning and Spatial Visualization

Students using the Singapore approach come to the middle grades with a thorough grounding in geometric relationships. They have had many experiences with angle concepts, properties of quadrilaterals and triangles, and relating nets to solid figures. Now, in the middle grades, the emphasis turns to area, volume, and representing figures on the coordinate plane.

In Course 1, students learn to use the basic formula for the area of a rectangle to construct (or derive) formulas for other figures, such as triangles, trapezoids, regular polygons, and circles. These formulas are then applied to finding the surface areas and volumes of prisms and pyramids.

In Course 2, work with surface area and volume will be extended from prisms and pyramids to cylinders, cones, and spheres. Students will begin working with parallel lines and transversals, as well as exploring their first compass-straightedge constructions.

Singapore Math covers identification, classification, and naming properties, while also providing students with critical opportunities to apply those properties in problem-solving situations or new contexts. The next few pages illustrate some of the application experiences that students will have as they continue to expand their abilities in geometric reasoning.

Geometry in the Coordinate Plane

In grade 5, students learned that an ordered pair describes a location on the coordinate plane. In middle school, students develop an awareness of coordinates as a way to describe relationships and quantify the properties of plane figures.

Example 1 Solving Real-World Problems

A plan for a rectangular playground is drawn in meters on a coordinate grid. Find the area and perimeter of the garden.

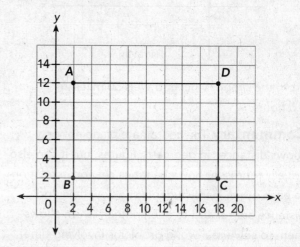

Length: $BC = 18 - 2 = 16$ m
Width: $AB = 12 - 2 = 10$ m

Perimeter: $16 + 16 + 10 + 10 = 52$ m
Area: $16 \cdot 10 = 160$ m²

Commentary Students should view the coordinate plane as a practical problem-solving tool. In this example, they can subtract coordinates to find side measures, and then apply the results to compute perimeter and area. When finding length, coordinates are restricted to the first quadrant, since operations with integers are not developed until grade 7.

Example 2 Graphing Equations

Vincent is riding his moped. He travels 20 miles per hour. How far does he travel in 2.5 hours?

Plot the graph of the data for the first 3 hours.

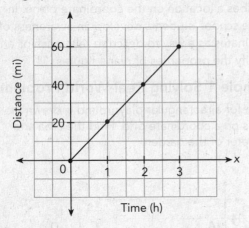

From the graph, Vincent travels 50 miles in 2.5 hours.

Commentary The coordinate plane not only shows distances in geometry figures, but it can also visually represent how quantities change in relation to each other. Here students see how time and distance are related to one another, which allows them to solve real-world problems involving time, distance, and speed. Students should understand that these are two very different but valid uses of the coordinate plane.

As the chapter on coordinate geometry concludes, students begin to see the coordinate plane as a way to integrate algebraic equations with geometric relationships. This idea will be developed and extended in Courses 2 and 3.

Areas of Polygons

Students' first experiences with area begin in Grade 3 as they compare the area of plane figures using different square units. In Grade 4, formulas for area and perimeter are introduced for rectangles and squares. Grade 5 focuses on triangle areas. Now area is extended to include quadrilaterals without right angles (parallelograms and trapezoids) and then other polygons and composite figures.

Composing and decomposing figures is a key idea in developing area concepts; for example, students will work with models to understand *why* the formula for the area of a triangle works.

Example 3 Area of a Triangle

Show that the area of a non-right triangle is one-half the area of a rectangle with the same base and height.

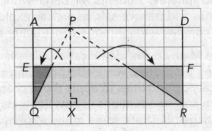

Area of triangle PQR = Sum of the areas within $EFRQ$

$$= QR \cdot \frac{1}{2} PX$$

$$= \frac{1}{2} QR \cdot PX$$

$$= \frac{1}{2} bh$$

Commentary Modeling reinforces problem-solving and spatial-reasoning skills in a way that formulas alone cannot. In this hands-on activity, students see visually and concretely that all triangles, not just right triangles, are half the area of the associated rectangle.

Example 4 Applying Area Formulas

The area of trapezoid JKLM is 3,000 square inches. Find the area of triangle JLM.

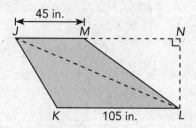

Area $JKLM = \frac{1}{2} h(b_1 + b_2)$

$= \frac{1}{2} NL(JM + KL)$

$= \frac{1}{2} NL(45 + 105)$

$= 75\ NL$

$75 \cdot NL = 3,000\ \text{in.}^2$

$NL = 40\ \text{in.}$

Area of triangle $JLM = \frac{1}{2} bh$

$= \frac{1}{2}(45 \cdot 40)$

$= 900\ \text{in.}^2$

Commentary In this example, students first must find the height of triangle JML, working backwards from the area of the trapezoid. Applying geometric reasoning and algebraic skills to two-step problems help students develop the perseverance needed to be successful mathematically.

Example 5 Parts to Wholes

The shaded area is 8.2 square inches. Find the area of the regular pentagon.

The shaded area represents one tenth the area of the pentagon, so the pentagon's area is $8.2 \cdot 10 = 82\ \text{in.}^2$

Commentary Students learn about the areas of regular polygons by seeing them as a combination of congruent triangles. Looking for these part-to-whole relationships helps students find the areas of other polygons.

Measures for Circles

Extending area concepts from polygons to circles, students will encounter the irrational number pi (π). Once the formulas for circumference and area are developed, students apply them to new problems.

Example 6 Relating Circles to Arcs

A quadrant of a circle is cut from a square. The side length of the square is 15 meters. Find the length of the arc of this quadrant. Use 3.14 for π.

Circumference $= 2\pi r$

$\approx 2 \cdot 3.14 \cdot 15$

$\approx 94.2\ \text{m}$

Length of each arc of the quadrant $\approx \frac{1}{4} \cdot 94.2$

$\approx 23.55\ \text{m}$

The length of the arc of this quadrant is about 23.55 meters.

Commentary Students know that a quadrant is one-quarter of a circle. They combine that knowledge with the circumference formula to solve this problem.

Measures for Solid Shapes

Calculating surface area and volume may be new to students, as earlier grades concentrated on properties of solids and their parts—faces, edges, and vertices. In Course 1 students find the surface area and volume of prisms and pyramids, which is extended to cylinders, cones, and spheres in Course 2. Visualization is key in the Singapore approach to surface area and volume. Nets are used to find surface area. The idea of uniform cross-sections helps students see why the volume of any prism equals the area of the base times the height.

Example 7 Surface Area and Nets

A rectangular prism is 8 centimeters tall, 5 centimeters wide, and 2 centimeters deep. Find its surface area.

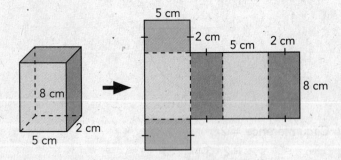

The total area of the vertical faces is equal to the area of a rectangle of length $(5 + 2 + 5 + 2)$ centimeters and width 8 centimeters.

Area of four vertical faces
$= 14 \cdot 8 = 112$ cm²

Area of two bases
$= 2 \cdot (5 \cdot 2) = 20$ cm²

Surface area of prism
$= 112 + 20 = 132$ cm²

Commentary This type of problem emphasizes the relationships between two-dimensional and three-dimensional figures. Students will later learn the formulas for surface areas for common solid figures.

Example 8 Real-World Problems

Find the volume of the prism.

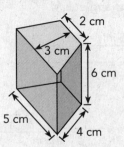

The base of the prism is a trapezoid. To find the volume of the prism, find the area of the trapezoidal base and multiply it by the height of the prism.

$$
\begin{aligned}
\text{Area of base} &= \frac{1}{2} h(b_1 + b_2) \\
&= \frac{1}{2} \cdot 3(2 + 5) \\
&= 10.5 \text{ cm}^2
\end{aligned}
$$

$$
\begin{aligned}
\text{Volume} &= Bh \\
&= 10.5 \cdot 6 \\
&= 63 \text{ cm}^3
\end{aligned}
$$

Commentary In the final lesson of the chapter on surface area and volume, students synthesize what they have learned about nets, surface area, and volume and apply it to problem-solving situations involving formulas.

Additional Teaching Resource

For additional reading, see *The Singapore Model Method for Learning Mathematics* published by the Ministry of Education of Singapore and *Bar Modeling: A Problem-solving Tool* by Yeap Ban Har, published by Marshall Cavendish Education.

Statistics and Probability (SP)

Models for Statistics and Inference

Students using Singapore mathematics are accustomed to modeling. They have used bars to model part-whole relationships and coordinate graphs to model two-variable equations. To prepare students to eventually create their own statistical models, Course 1 begins with the most common and useful statistical graphs. These give a visual interpretation to the measures of central tendency—mean, median, and mode—and introduce students in a gradual way to the meaning of a data distribution.

Methods of collecting, organizing, and analyzing data were introduced using graphs, such as line plots, and line graphs, in Grades 3 through 5. In this course, dot plots and histograms are added to students' toolbox of data displays. Here, for the first time, they are taught that the shape of the data has meaning. In Courses 2 and 3, students will learn how to use box-and-whisker plots and scatter plots to analyze data sets.

As students work with data displays, they will also learn the basic numerical methods of data analysis. They computed mean, median, and mode in Grade 4. In this course, they see how these measures of center are related in symmetric and skewed distributions. Measures of spread and variability in this course are confined to the range of a data set. Course 2 contains a major focus on variability, with topics such as interquartile range and mean absolute deviation. Probability, introduced with simple events in Grades 4 and 5, will return in Course 2 with a complete chapter on probability models and distributions.

Graphical Data Displays

The most basic tool for organizing data is the table. Students begin with tables that use tally marks to show responses to survey questions. As they count the tallies, they are finding frequency, an idea given visual form in histograms (for large data sets) and dot plots (for smaller data sets).

Example 1 Collecting and Tabulating Data

The local library asked a random group of teenagers how often they visited the library in a month. A tally chart was used to record the findings.

Visits per Month	Tally	Frequency
0–5	~~HHt~~ //	
6–10	~~HHt~~ ~~HHt~~ ~~HHt~~ ////	
More than 10	////	

Complete the frequency column in the chart. How many teenagers were surveyed?

First row: 7 tallies
Second row: 19 tallies
Third row: 4 tallies

Total teenagers surveyed: 7 + 19 + 4 = 30

There were 30 teenagers in this survey.

Commentary With so many ways of displaying data, students can miss the basic underlying idea, the reason for collecting and displaying data in the first place: Data sets are used to make decisions or predictions. Working with tally charts for surveys helps to reinforce the real-world motivations for collecting data.

Example 2 Histograms for Displays of Grouped Data

This data set shows the ages of people visiting a senior center one evening.

67, 63, 54, 66, 66, 68, 60, 62, 67, 64, 73, 54, 67, 70, 58, 64, 66, 55, 59, 68, 70, 66, 65, 65, 62, 55, 68, 61, 65, 50, 60, 61, 66, 63, 66, 59, 57, 69, 56, 53

Group the data into 3 intervals and into 6 intervals. Draw a histogram for each grouping. Compare the two histograms.

Students first construct the frequency tables, making sure their intervals are of equal size.

Age (yr)	50–57	58–65	66–73
Frequency	8	16	16

Age	50–53	54–57	58–61	62–65	66–69	70–73
Freq.	2	6	7	9	13	3

The tables are used to draw the histograms.

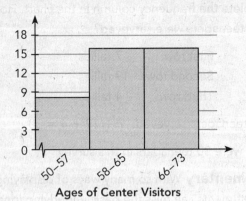

Ages of Center Visitors

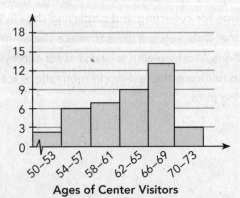

Ages of Center Visitors

The 3-interval histogram is easier than the 6-interval histogram to group and draw. But the shape and spread of the data is shown better in the 6-interval histogram.

Commentary This may be students' first experience with displaying grouped data. Initially, students are told how many intervals to group data into. By comparing the displays when two interval sizes are used, they can see that very different histograms may result. In later courses, students will use graphing calculators to easily experiment with intervals of different sizes.

Measures of Central Tendency

A major emphasis of this course is on calculating mean, median, and mode. Students use these measures to solve problems and describe data sets with a variety of characteristics.

Example 3 The Mean and Missing Data

Alex wants to have at least an 85 mean score in math this quarter. His first five test scores are 85, 90, 75, 80, and 85. What score does he need on the sixth test, which is the last test, to meet his goal?

Total of 6 tests = mean × number of scores
$$= 85 × 6$$
$$= 510$$

First 5 test scores = 85 + 90 + 75 + 80 + 85
$$= 415$$

Difference = 510 − 415
$$= 95$$

Alex needs a score of 95 on the last test.

Commentary One problem type not often encountered in traditional programs involves using the mean to identify the total. Once the total is found, it can be used to identify a missing data item. This type of problem is frequently found on standardized tests.

Example 4 Finding Mean from Dot Plots

There are six pitchers of lemonade at a big family picnic. The dot plot shows the size of each pitcher in quarts. Each dot represents 1 pitcher. Find the mean number of quarts for these pitchers.

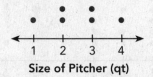

Size of Pitcher (qt)

1 one-quart pitcher:	$1 \cdot 1 = 1$ qt
2 two-quart pitchers:	$2 \cdot 2 = 4$ qt
2 three-quart pitchers:	$2 \cdot 3 = 6$ qt
1 four-quart pitcher:	$1 \cdot 4 = 4$ qt

Mean = total quarts ÷ number of pitchers

$$= \frac{1 + 4 + 6 + 4}{6}$$

$$= \frac{15}{6}$$

$$= 2\frac{1}{2}$$

The mean size of the pitchers is $2\frac{1}{2}$ quarts.

Commentary Example 4 illustrates finding the mean. The median can also be found using a dot plot, because the dot plot orders the data. The data is divided in two halves. The middle item (or the mean of the two middle items) is the median.

Example 5 Using Mode to Summarize Data

A number of people were asked if they checked their email every day. The answer choices were always (A), sometimes (S), and never (N). Use the mode to summarize this data.

A, S, S, S, S, N, A, S, S, S, A, S, A, A, A, S, S, S, N, A, A, N, S, S, A, S, S, N, A, A, N

10 people responded "Always," 15 people responded "Sometimes,' and 5 people responded "Never."

The mode is "Sometimes."

Commentary Since the data set is not numeric, the mean and the median cannot be found. However, the responses can be counted and the mode determined. This type of data set might be displayed with a bar graph.

Example 6 Comparing Mean and Median

A survey asked the number of video games that were purchased in the previous month. This dot plot shows the survey results. Each dot represents one person who was surveyed.

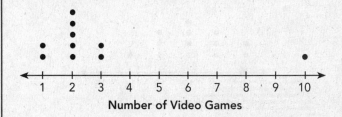

Number of Video Games

Find the mean and median. Which of the two measures of central tendency better describes the data set?

mean = total games ÷ total people

$$= \frac{(2 \cdot 1) + (5 \cdot 2) + (2 \cdot 3) + (1 \cdot 10)}{10}$$

$$= \frac{28}{10}$$

$$= 2.8$$

The mean is 2.8 games.

There are 10 people in the survey. The fifth and sixth people are in the middle. They each bought 2 games. So, the median is 2 games.

The mean is 2.8 games. However, most of the people bought 2 video games or fewer in the previous month. So, the median describes the data better than the mean.

Commentary Representing this data on the dot plot helps students see how the outlier at 10 pulls the mean to the right. If the person who bought 10 games had bought even more, the mean would increase but the median and mode would not change.

Symmetric and Skewed Data

The mean, median, and mode are ways to describe the center of a data set, and students find how to use dot plots to obtain these measures. Dot plots can also help students describe distributions of data. They are introduced to the difference between symmetric and skewed distributions, and relate the measures of center to these distributions.

Example 7 Symmetrical Distributions

The dot plot shows the weights, in ounces, of some packages mailed during one week. Each dot represents one package.

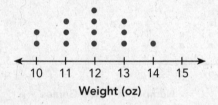

Weight (oz)

Find the mean, median, and mode of the data.

mean = total weight ÷ number of packages

$$= \frac{20 + 33 + 48 + 39 + 14}{13}$$

$$= \frac{154}{13}$$

$$\approx 11.85 \text{ oz}$$

mode   Packages weighing 12 ounces were shipped most often.

median   The seventh item of data of these 13 items is the median. The median weight is 12 ounces.

Commentary Example 7 shows a data distribution that is nearly symmetrical about a vertical line through the center. In this type of distribution, the mean, mode, and median are almost the same.

Example 8 Skewed Distributions

The dot plot shows the number of miles walked by some students raising money for charity. Each dot represents one student.

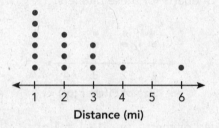

Distance (mi)

Find the mean, median, and mode.

mean = total miles ÷ total walkers

$$= \frac{6 + 8 + 9 + 4 + 6}{15}$$

$$= \frac{33}{15}$$

$$= 2.2 \text{ mi}$$

mode   The 1-mile distance was walked by the greatest number of students. The mode is 1 mile.

median   The eighth item of data of these 15 items is the median. The median distance is 2 miles.

Commentary In contrast to Example 7, this data distribution is skewed to the right. The data are clustered at one end of the range. In this type of distribution, the median will tell students what is most typical of the data, but the mean will help them take into account extreme values.

Additional Teaching Resource

For additional reading, see *The Singapore Model Method for Learning Mathematics* published by the Ministry of Education of Singapore and *Bar Modeling: A Problem-solving Tool* by Yeap Ban Har, published by Marshall Cavendish Education.

Find Factors of a Whole Number

TEACHING STRATEGY

1. **Vocabulary** Make sure students understand the term *factor*. Remind them that factors are numbers that are multiplied together to find a product. Also point out that a factor of a number divides that number without a remainder.

2. **Teach** Direct students to Step 1 of Example 1. **Ask** What is the least number of factors a whole number can have? [two, 1 and itself] Direct students to Step 2 of Example 1. **Ask** Why is 5 not a factor of 36? [36 ÷ 5 has a remainder, 7 R1. Factors divide a number without a remainder.] Point out to students that when the factor pairs start to repeat, then all the factors have been found. Remind them to list the factors from least to greatest. Direct students to Example 2. Tell them they can use division facts to check the factors of 36 in Example 1 as well as use multiplication facts to check the factors of 54 in Example 2.

3. **Quick Check** Look for these common errors as students solve the Quick Check exercises.
   - Incorrectly listing multiples instead of factors indicating a misunderstanding of the vocabulary and concept.
   - Omitting some factors, demonstrating carelessness creating a list of factors.
   - Listing incorrect factors, showing a lack of proficiency with basic multiplication and division facts.

4. **Next Steps** Assign the practice exercises to students who show understanding. For students who need more support, provide tutoring using the alternate teaching strategy.

Additional Teaching Resource
🖱 Online Transition Guide with Reteach and Extra Practice worksheets from previous grade levels

ALTERNATE INTERVENTION STRATEGY

Materials: TRT12 (Graph Paper)

Strategy: Graph the factors for a given number.

1. Have students use graph paper to find factors by picturing all the rectangular arrays that are possible for a given number.

2. Tell students that you are going to identify the factors of 18. Draw a 1-by-18 array. Write 1 × 18 = 18. Point out that 1 and 18 are both factors of 18. **Ask** What other rectangular arrays can 18 squares be arranged into? [2 by 9, 3 by 6] Draw the array and add the dimensions of each array to your list of factors.

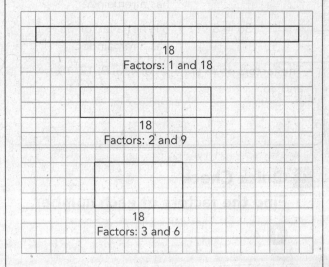

18
Factors: 1 and 18

18
Factors: 2 and 9

18
Factors: 3 and 6

3. When students have exhausted all possible arrays or rectangles, they have found the factors of the number. Remind them to list the factors in order from least to greatest. **Ask** What are the factors of 18? [1, 2, 3, 6, 9, and 18]

4. Continue with other numbers that have factors less than 20. In each case, for every array write a multiplication fact and identify the factors involved.

Find Factors of a Whole Number

Example 1 — Use multiplication to find factors

STEP 1 Use multiplication facts to find the factors of a number. Start with 1.

$36 = 1 \cdot 36$

STEP 2 Identify other factor pairs and continue until factors repeat.

$36 = 2 \cdot 18$
$36 = 3 \cdot 12$
$36 = 4 \cdot 9$
$36 = 5 \cdot ?$ 5 is not a factor. $36 \div 5$ has a remainder.
$36 = 6 \cdot 6$
$36 = 7 \cdot ?$ 7 is not a factor. $36 \div 7$ has a remainder.
$36 = 8 \cdot ?$ 8 is not a factor. $36 \div 8$ has a remainder.

The factors of 36 are 1, 2, 3, 4, 6, 9, 12, 18, and 36.

Example 2 — Use division to find factors

Find the factors of 54.

STEP 1 Use division facts to find the factors of a number. Start with 1.

$54 \div 1 = 54$

STEP 2 Identify other factor pairs and continue until factors repeat.

$54 \div 2 = 27$
$54 \div 3 = 18$
$54 \div 4 = ?$ $54 \div 4$ has a remainder. 4 is not a factor.
$54 \div 5 = ?$ $54 \div 5$ has a remainder. 5 is not a factor.
$54 \div 6 = 9$
$54 \div 7 = ?$ $36 \div 7$ has a remainder. 7 is not a factor.
$54 \div 8 = ?$ $36 \div 8$ has a remainder. 8 is not a factor.

The factors of 36 are 1, 2, 3, 6, 9, 18, 27, and 54.

✓ Quick Check

Find the factors of each number.

1 6 _____

2 9 _____

3 10 _____

4 42 _____

Practice on Your Own
Find the factors of each number.

5 39 _____

6 77 _____

7 96 _____

8 35 _____

9 100 _____

10 144 _____

Find Multiples of a Whole Number

TEACHING STRATEGY

1. **Vocabulary** Make sure students understand the term *multiple*. Remind them that a multiple is the product of the given number and a whole number besides zero. Emphasize that zero should not be used when finding multiples of numbers.

2. **Teach** Direct students to Example 1. Have students count by 2 aloud starting with the number 2. **Ask** The numbers you just named are multiples of what number? [2] Direct students to Example 2. Point out to students that although they are writing the first five multiples of 8, they can find many more multiples. **Ask** What is the 10th multiple of 8? [80] How do you know? [8 · 10 = 80; The position of the multiple (10th) tells you what number to multiply 8 by.] Tell students they can use multiplication facts to check the multiples of 2 in Example 1 as well as use addition facts to check the multiples of 8 in Example 2.

3. **Quick Check** Look for these common errors as students solve the Quick Check exercises.
   - Incorrectly listing one multiple and thus writing all subsequent multiples incorrectly.
   - Lack of proficiency of addition facts leading to incorrect calculation of sums.
   - Lack of proficiency of multiplication facts leading to incorrect calculation of products.

4. **Next Steps** Assign the practice exercises to students who show understanding. For students who need more support, provide tutoring using the alternate teaching strategy.

Additional Teaching Resource

Online Transition Guide with Reteach and Extra Practice worksheets from previous grade levels

ALTERNATE INTERVENTION STRATEGY

Materials: TRT1 (Number Lines)

Strategy: Use a number line to find multiples.

1. Have students use number lines to find multiples of given numbers.

2. Demonstrate how to show multiples of 3. Have students begin on the point for 0, count by 3s, and draw equal jumps to the numbers as they count and name them.

3. Suggest students circle all the numbers they landed on. Explain that when they count by threes, the numbers they name are multiples of 3.

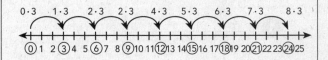

4. Now ask students to write the multiplication fact for each multiple. Have them write 1 · 3 above the 3, 2 · 3 over the 6, and so on.

5. Have students recall the definition of *multiple* and determine that 0 is not a multiple and that 3 is the first multiple of the number 3. Guide them to see that the other numbers they circled are multiples because they are the products of the number 3 and the whole numbers 1, 2, 3, 4, 5, 6, 7, and 8.

6. Repeat the activity for multiples of 4 and 5. When you feel the students understand how to find multiples of a number, have them find the first five multiples of other numbers using multiplication only.

Find Multiples of a Whole Number

Example 1 — Use repeated addition

Find the first five multiples of 2.

Count by 2 starting with the number 2.

$(+2)$ $(+2)$ $(+2)$ $(+2)$

2   4   6   8   10

The first five multiples of 2 are 2, 4, 6, 8, and 10.

Example 2 — Use division to find factors

Find the first 5 multiples of 8.

Use multiplication facts to find the first five multiples of 8.

Start by multiplying by 1.

$8 \cdot 1 = 8$
$8 \cdot 2 = 16$
$8 \cdot 3 = 24$
$8 \cdot 4 = 32$
$8 \cdot 5 = 40$

The first five multiples of 8 are 8, 16, 24, 32, 40.

☑ Quick Check

Find the first five multiples of each number.

1 3 _____

2 10 _____

3 16 _____

4 21 _____

Practice on Your Own
Find the first five multiples of each number.

5 5 _____

6 11 _____

7 15 _____

8 19 _____

9 25 _____

10 32 _____

11 45 _____

12 100 _____

13 111 _____

14 150 _____

15 250 _____

16 300 _____

17 500 _____

18 801 _____

19 1,000 _____

Identify Prime Numbers

TEACHING STRATEGY

1. **Vocabulary** Make sure students understand the meaning of the term *prime*. A prime number has only two different factors, 1 and the number itself. Remind students that a factor divides a number without a remainder. The number 1 is not prime as it does not have two different factors.

2. **Teach** Direct students to Step 1 of Example 1. **Ask** Why do you divide 13 by 2? [You divide to find out if 2 is a factor of 13.] Is 2 a factor of 13? [No.] How do you know? [2 does not divide 13 evenly. There is a remainder.] Direct students to Step 2 of Example 1. **Ask** Why do you stop dividing after testing 6? [You can stop dividing because the divisor and quotient, 2 and 6, repeat.] Direct students to Step 2 of Example 2. **Ask** Is 3 a factor of 15? [Yes; 3 divides 15 evenly, 3 · 5 = 15.] **Ask** Is 15 a prime number? [No; 15 has more than 2 factors.] Point out to students that once a factor other than 1 divides the number without a remainder, the number is not prime.

3. **Quick Check** Look for these common errors as students solve the Quick Check exercises.
   - Reaching incorrect conclusions when dividing because they do not recall basic facts.
   - Mistakenly identify a number as prime because they have missed factors.
   - Stopping dividing too soon, before a divisor already tested is repeated as the quotient.
   - Listing 1 as a prime number.

4. **Next Steps** Assign the practice exercises to students who show understanding. For students who need more support, provide tutoring using the alternate teaching strategy.

Additional Teaching Resource
🖱 Online Transition Guide with Reteach and Extra Practice worksheets from previous grade levels

ALTERNATE INTERVENTION STRATEGY

Materials: grid paper

Strategy: Create rectangular arrays to determine whether a number is a prime number.

1. Tell students they can use graph paper to help them determine whether a number is a prime number.

2. Instruct them to shade 3 adjacent unit squares on the graph paper in the shape of a rectangle. Have them draw as many different rectangles as possible.

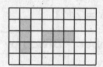

3. Discuss with students how the rectangles are shaped. Point out that in order to arrange three squares in the shape of a rectangle, you must either draw 1 column by 3 rows or 3 rows by 1 column. Pont out that the dimensions of these rectangles are 1 by 3 or 3 by 1. So, 3 and 1 are the only factors of 3. Tell students that a prime number, such as 3, can only have its unit squares arranged in a rectangle where either the length or the width is 1 unit.

4. Next, have students shade 6 adjacent unit squares in as many ways as possible, keeping them in the shape of a rectangle.

   Ask What arrangements were you able to make with six squares? [1 by 6, 6 by 1, 2 by 3, 3 by 2] Tell students that 6 is not a prime number because its factors are 1, 2, 3, and 6.

5. Have students shade unit squares representing the numbers 2, 4, 5, 7, 8, and 9. **Ask** Which of the numbers are prime? [2, 5, 7] Which of the numbers are not prime? [4, 8, 9]

Identify Prime Numbers

Example 1

Decide whether 13 is a prime number.

STEP 1 Divide to find possible factors.
Start with 2 to test whether it is a factor.

$13 \div 2 = 6$ R 1 2 is not a factor.
$13 \div 2$ has a remainder.

STEP 2 Continue testing factors. Record each result in a table. Stop dividing when a divisor and quotient repeat.

$13 \div 3 = 4$ R 1
$13 \div 4 = 3$ R 1
$13 \div 5 = 2$ R 3
$13 \div 6 = 2$ R 1

Number	Divide by	Remainder?
13	3	yes
13	4	yes
13	5	yes
13	6	yes

The only factors of 13 are 13 and 1. 13 is a prime number.

Example 2

Decide whether 15 is a prime number.

STEP 1 Divide to find possible factors.
Start with 2 to test whether it is a factor.

$15 \div 2 = 7$ R 1

STEP 2 Continue testing factors. Record each result in a table. Once you find that 15 is divisible by 3, you do not need to test other factors. If a number has a factor besides itself and 1, it is not prime.

$15 \div 3 = 5$

Number	Divide by	Remainder?
15	3	no

The factors of 15 are 1, 3, 5, and 15. 15 is not a prime number.

✔ Quick Check
Identify all the prime numbers from the following set of numbers.

1 8, 12, 17

_____

2 10, 19, 20

_____

3 1, 2, 5, 10

_____

4 23, 33, 90

_____

Practice on Your Own
Identify all the prime numbers from the following set of numbers.

5 7, 12, 25, 46

_____

6 19, 43, 121, 137

_____

7 13, 27, 81, 28

_____

8 18, 21, 31, 83

_____

9 1, 17, 37, 61

_____

10 58, 69, 98, 117

_____

Use Order of Operations to Simplify an Expression

TEACHING STRATEGY

1. **Vocabulary** Explain to students that the *order of operations* is a set of rules telling us which operations to carry out first when an expression involves more than one operation.

2. **Teach** Direct students to Example 1. Demonstrate why having a set of rules is necessary by working out the problem from left to right instead of using the correct order of operations. $(9 - 2 \cdot 3 = 7 \cdot 3 = 21)$ **Ask** Do you get the same answer? [No.] Direct students to Examples 2 and 3. **Ask** How are the expressions in Examples 2 and 3 different from the expression in Example 1? [The expressions in Examples 2 and 3 include parentheses.] In those expressions, what do you need to do first?{perform the operations inside parentheses.] Before working through Examples 2 and 3, ask a volunteer to list the operations they see in each problem, in the order in which they would be performed.

3. **Quick Check** Look for these common errors as students solve the Quick Check exercises.
   - Always working from left to right and forgetting to consider parentheses.
   - Incorrectly working from right to left, leading to miscalculation.

4. **Next Steps** Assign the practice exercises to students who show understanding. For students who need more support, provide tutoring using the alternate teaching strategy.

Additional Teaching Resource

 Online Transition Guide with Reteach and Extra Practice worksheets from previous grade levels

ALTERNATE INTERVENTION STRATEGY

Materials: 25 colored cubes

Strategy: Use concrete manipulatives to model simplifying expressions using the order of operations.

1. Tell students you are going to solve a problem involving cubes. **Ask** If I have 5 cubes and then Student 1, Student 2, and Student 3 each give me 2 cubes, how many cubes will I have? [11] **Ask** What is an expression that describes this problem? [$5 + 3 \cdot 2$] If we solve this problem from left to right, without paying attention to the order of operations, what value do we get? [16]

2. Now, demonstrate using cubes. Ask students to take on the roles of Students 1, 2, and 3 from the problem and follow it exactly. Discuss with them why you only have 11 cubes and not 16. Lead students to conclude that multiplication comes before addition, unless parentheses in the expression indicate otherwise.

3. Act out and solve the following problems. In each case, discuss whether parentheses are needed.

   I have 2 cubes. Student 1 has 25 cubes that she divides equally between 4 other students and myself. **Ask** When I get my share, how many cubes will I have? [$2 + 25 \div 5 = 7$; parentheses are not needed]

   I have 25 cubes and I give 9 of them to Student 1 before I share the ones I have left with 4 other students. **Ask** How many cubes do I have now?
   [$(25 - 9) \div 4 = 4$; parentheses are needed.]

   I have 25 cubes and I give 3 of them to each of 4 students. **Ask** How many cubes do I have now? [$25 - 3 \cdot 4 = 13$; parentheses are not needed.]

Use Order of Operations to Simplify an Expression

The correct order of operations:

STEP 1 Work inside parentheses.

STEP 2 Multiply and divide from left to right.

STEP 3 Add and subtract from left to right.

Example 1

Simplify $9 - 2 \cdot 3$.

$$9 - 6$$
$$3$$

Example 2

Simplify $(8 + 10) \div 3$

$$18 \div 3$$
$$6$$

Example 3

Simplify $(30 - 18) + 6 \cdot 9$

$$12 + 6 \cdot 9$$
$$12 + 54$$
$$66$$

✔ Quick Check
Simplify.

1 $(25 + 5) - 3 \cdot 10$

2 $20 \cdot (16 \div 4) - 15$

3 $12 \cdot 7 + 28 \div 4$

4 $80 - (60 \div 5) \cdot 6$

Practice on Your Own
Simplify.

5 $100 \div 20 + 50 \cdot 3$

6 $\dfrac{16 \cdot 2}{8} + 4 \cdot 6$

7 $(5 \cdot 2) + (8 - 3)$

8 $8 \cdot 5 + 33 \cdot 2$

9 $(18 + 18) - \dfrac{16 - 1}{5}$

10 $(60 - 21) - 5 \cdot 7$

11 $210 - (20 + 5) \cdot 8$

12 $42 \cdot 5 + 48 \div 3$

13 $15 \cdot (77 \div 7) + 35$

NS SKILL 5 Represent Positive Numbers on a Number Line

TEACHING STRATEGY

1. **Vocabulary** Make sure students understand the term *interval* as it pertains to a number line. **Ask** If I need to show sevenths on a number line, how many intervals will be between each whole number? [7]

2. **Teach** Draw a number line on the board and place 11 tick marks, evenly spaced, on the line. Do not label any of the tick marks. **Ask** Without any labels, is it possible to determine what the tick marks represent? [No.] Add the labels 0 to 10 to the number line beneath the appropriate tick marks. **Ask** According to the labels, how is the line divided? [Possible answer: Each tick mark represents one unit on the line. Each tick mark represents a whole on the line.] Add a single smaller tick mark halfway between each pair of numbers. **Ask** What do these new marks represent? [halves] Stress that a number line can be divided in any way that is convenient as long as it is appropriately labeled. Review the Examples with students, making sure they understand how to correctly divide up the number line in each case. You also may want to draw vertical number lines, so that students get sufficient practice with both types of lines.

3. **Quick Check** Look for these common errors as students solve the Quick Check exercises.

   • Mislabeling numbers on the number line.
   • Incorrectly dividing the number line into the appropriate intervals for the number set.

4. **Next Steps** Assign the practice exercises to students who show understanding. For students who need more support, provide tutoring using the alternate teaching strategy.

Additional Teaching Resource
📀 Online Transition Guide with Reteach and Extra Practice worksheets from previous grade levels

ALTERNATE INTERVENTION STRATEGY

Materials: several decks of playing cards, TRT1 (Number Lines)

Strategy: Plot numbers on a number line.

1. Have students work in pairs. Give each pair a deck of cards and ask them to remove all the face cards (jacks, queens, kings, and jokers).

2. Explain that the value of each card is the number face on the card. Each ace has a value of 1.

3. Draw a number line like the one below.

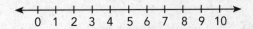

4. Have each student draw a card from the deck and place a point on his or her number line where that number value belongs. Have students continue until each has plotted 5 numbers.

5. Repeat the process using decimals. Draw a number line from 1 to 10 divided into decimal tenths. Have students remove the 10s from their decks. They should draw 2 cards this time. The first card is the ones value and the second card is the tenths. Students should plot points on the number line to indicate the numbers they draw.

6. Repeat the process one more time using fractions. Have students remove the 6s, 7s, 8s, and 9s from their decks. In this exercise, students draw 2 cards and write a proper fraction using the numbers they draw. For example, if a student draws 3 and 5, he or she writes the fraction $\frac{3}{5}$.

7. Have students draw their own number lines with the appropriate labels and plot a point to indicate the fraction. If students are having difficulty drawing number lines to represent fractions, you may want to provide examples of number lines from 0 to 1 divided into halves, thirds, fourths, and fifths.

Represent Positive Numbers on a Number Line

Example 1 **Whole Numbers**

Draw a horizontal number line to represent the even numbers from 15 to 25.

STEP 1 Draw a number line starting at 15 and ending at 25.

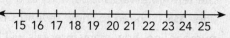

STEP 2 Plot points at each even number.

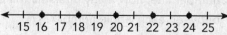

Example 2 **Fractions**

Draw a horizontal number line to represent fractions from 0 to 1 with an interval of $\frac{1}{5}$.

STEP 1 Draw a number line starting at 0 and ending at 1. The interval is $\frac{1}{5}$ so the number line should be divided into 5 equal intervals.

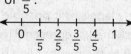

STEP 2 Plot points for each fraction.

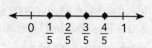

Example 3 **Decimals**

Draw a horizontal number line to represent decimals between 5 and 6 with an interval of 0.2.

STEP 1 Draw a number line starting at 5 and ending at 6. The interval is 0.2 so include 5.2, 5.4, 5.6, and 5.8.

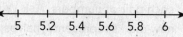

STEP 2 Plot points for each decimal.

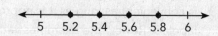

✔ Quick Check

Draw a horizontal number line to represent each set of numbers.

1 Even numbers from 1 to 10.

2 Decimals from 4 to 5 with an interval of 0.25.

3 Fractions between 0 and 1 with an interval of $\frac{1}{3}$.

Practice on Your Own
Draw a horizontal number line to represent each set of numbers.

4 Mixed numbers from 1 to 3 with an interval of $\frac{1}{4}$.

5 Even numbers from 10 to 20.

6 Decimals between 10 and 11 with an interval of 0.1.

Write Statements of Inequality Using > and <

TEACHING STRATEGY

1. **Vocabulary** Review the symbols > (is greater than) and < (is less than) with students. Have volunteers describe methods they use to distinguish the symbols, such as the pointed end always aims towards the lesser number.

2. **Teach** Remind students that fractions and decimals are different ways of writing numbers. Review the Examples with students. **Ask** How does a number line help you compare numbers? [Possible answer: You can compare the numbers' positions. The number further to the right (or higher up on a vertical number line) is the greater number.] When reviewing Example 2, point out that there are other ways to compare two fractions with unlike denominators. **Ask** When you compare two fractions with like denominators, what part of each fraction do you look at? Explain. [Possible answer: You look at the numerators. The fraction with the greater numerator has the greater value when both fractions name the same whole.] Explain that you can multiply the numerator and denominator of $\frac{1}{4}$ by 2 to write the equivalent fraction $\frac{2}{8}$.

   Now students can compare the fractions $\frac{2}{8}$ and $\frac{3}{8}$ by comparing the numerators.

3. **Quick Check** Look for these common errors as students solve the Quick Check exercises.
   - Confusing the > and < symbols.
   - Mistakenly comparing just the numerators when two fractions have unlike denominators.

4. **Next Steps** Assign the practice exercises to students who show understanding. For students who need more support, provide tutoring using the alternate teaching strategy.

Additional Teaching Resource

Online Transition Guide with Reteach and Extra Practice worksheets from previous grade levels

ALTERNATE INTERVENTION STRATEGY

Materials: none

Strategy: Use bar models to compare fractions and decimals.

1. Write the fractions $\frac{2}{3}$ and $\frac{5}{6}$ on the board. Tell students you are going to use bar models to compare the values of the fractions.

2. Draw a model for $\frac{2}{3}$ and one for $\frac{5}{6}$. **Ask** Which model has more area shaded? [The model for $\frac{5}{6}$.] Which fraction is greater? $\left[\frac{5}{6}\right]$ Write $\frac{2}{3} < \frac{5}{6}$ on the board below the models.

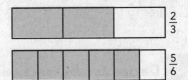

3. Repeat the exercise for 0.35 and 0.4. Draw bar models for the decimals and have students write an inequality for the numbers based on which model has more area shaded.

4. Repeat the exercise a final time for 0.2 and $\frac{1}{4}$.

   Do not convert the fraction to a decimal. Instead, draw models for the decimal and fraction that represent equal sized wholes. Allow students to compare the decimal amount shaded to the fractional amount shaded to see that $0.2 < \frac{1}{4}$.

5. Help students connect the models to a number line, showing how the lines between each part in the model can represent tick marks on a number line. Work through the three examples above with students, now using a number line to help them compare the values.

Write Statements of Inequality Using > and <

Example 1 Decimals

Compare 0.26 and 0.3 using > or <.

STEP 1 Draw a number line to help compare the numbers.

STEP 2 Locate both numbers on the number line.

0.26 lies to the left of 0.3. So 0.26 < 0.3.

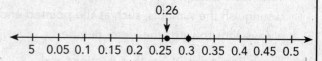

Example 2 Fractions

Compare $\frac{3}{8}$ and $\frac{1}{4}$ using > or <.

STEP 1 Draw a number line to show fourths and another to show eighths. Align the whole numbers.

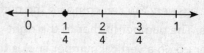

STEP 2 Locate the fractions on each number line.

$\frac{3}{8}$ lies to the right of $\frac{1}{4}$. So $\frac{3}{8} > \frac{1}{4}$.

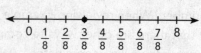

Example 3 Decimals and Fractions

Compare 0.55 and $\frac{3}{5}$ using > or <.

STEP 1 Convert $\frac{3}{5}$ to a decimal. $\frac{3}{5}$ = 5 0.6

STEP 2 Draw a number line and locate the numbers.

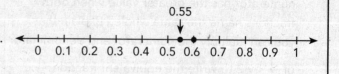

0.55 lies to the left of 06. So 0.55 < $\frac{3}{5}$.

✓ Quick Check

Compare each pair of numbers using > or <. Use a number line to help you.

1 1.05 ? 1.9

2 $\frac{2}{3}$? $\frac{5}{6}$

3 0.9 ? $\frac{7}{10}$

Practice on Your Own

Compare each pair of numbers using > or <. Use a number line to help you.

4 6.95 ? 6.59

5 $\frac{3}{4}$? 0.79

6 $\frac{3}{7}$? $\frac{5}{9}$

7 $\frac{5}{6}$? $\frac{7}{8}$

8 2.905 ? 2.95

5 0.4 < $\frac{1}{3}$

Add and Subtract Decimals

TEACHING STRATEGY

1. **Vocabulary** Make sure students understand the terms *regroup* and *rename*.

2. **Teach** Point out that adding and subtracting decimals follows the same rules used for whole numbers. Make sure they understand the importance of writing the problem vertically in order to line up the decimal points. Show students how misaligning the numbers can result in computation errors, using Example 1 as a model:

$$
\begin{array}{r}
3.9 \\
\times\ 2.45 \\
\hline
2.84
\end{array}
$$

Ask In Example 1, why do you need to regroup in Step 3? [You are adding 9 tenths and 4 tenths, which is equal to 13 tenths. You need to regroup 13 tenths as 1 one and 3 tenths.] In Example 2, why do you need to regroup in Step 1? [You are trying to subtract 5 hundredths from 0 hundredths, which you cannot do. So you need to regroup 1 tenth as 10 hundredths.]

3. **Quick Check** Look for these common errors as students solve the Quick Check exercises.
   - Forgetting to align decimal points, or misaligning them, when adding or subtracting.
   - Incorrectly regrouping and/or renaming when adding or subtracting.

   These errors indicate a lack of understanding of place value.

4. **Next Steps** Assign the practice exercises to students who show understanding. For students who need more support, provide tutoring using the alternate teaching strategy.

Additional Teaching Resource
Online Transition Guide with Reteach and Extra Practice worksheets from previous grade levels

ALTERNATE INTERVENTION STRATEGY

Materials: play money in denominations of dollars, dimes, and pennies

Strategy: Use manipulatives to add and subtract decimals.

1. Write 3.46 + 2.35 on the board.

2. Distribute the play money. Explain to students that the dollar bills represent the ones, the dimes represent the tenths, and the pennies represent the hundredths. Model each number.

3. Tell students you will start by adding the hundredths. **Ask** How many pennies are there in all? [6 + 5 = 11] Explain that you must now regroup since you have more than 10 pennies. Model regrouping for students by taking 10 pennies and trading them for 1 dime. Next, add the tenths. **Ask** How many dimes are there in all? [4 + 3 + 1 = 8] Finally, add the ones. **Ask** How many dollars are there in all? [3 + 2 = 5] What is the sum of 3.46 and 2.35? [5.81]

4. Work through a subtraction problem with students: 4.05 − 2.73. Model 4.05 with 4 dollars and 5 pennies. Tell students you will start by subtracting the hundredths. Subtract 3 hundredths from 5 hundredths by removing 3 of the 5 pennies. **Ask** How many pennies are left? [2] Next, subtract the tenths. **Ask** Why do we need to regroup before we can subtract the tenths? [You cannot take 7 tenths away from 0 tenths.] Model regrouping by taking 1 of the dollars and exchanging it for 10 dimes. Then take away 7 of the 10 dimes. **Ask** How many dimes are left? [3] Finally, subtract the ones. Take away 2 of the 3 dollars. **Ask** How many dollars are left? [1] What is the difference of 4.05 and 2.73? [1.32]

Add and Subtract Decimals

Example 1 Add Decimals

Find the value of 3.9 + 2.45.

STEP 1 Rewrite the problem vertically in order to align the decimal points in each number. Add a zero to 3.9 as a placeholder.

$$\begin{array}{r} 3.90 \\ +\ 2.45 \\ \hline \end{array}$$

STEP 2 Begin by adding the digits in the hundredths place.

$$\begin{array}{r} 3.90 \\ +\ 2.45 \\ \hline 5 \end{array}$$

STEP 3 Add the digits in the tenths place. Since 9 + 4 = 13, regroup 10 tenths as 1 one.

$$\begin{array}{r} \overset{1}{3}.90 \\ +\ 2.45 \\ \hline 35 \end{array}$$

STEP 4 Place the decimal point in the answer. Add the digits in the ones place.

$$\begin{array}{r} \overset{1}{3}.90 \\ +\ 2.45 \\ \hline 6.35 \end{array}$$

3.9 + 2.45 = 6.35

Example 2 Subtract Decimals

Find the value of 8.6 − 4.55.

STEP 1 Rewrite the problem vertically in order to align the decimal points in each number. Add a zero to 8.6 as a placeholder.

$$\begin{array}{r} 8.60 \\ -\ 4.55 \\ \hline \end{array}$$

STEP 2 Begin by subtracting the digits in the hundredths place. Regroup 1 tenth as 10 hundreds so that you can subtract.

$$\begin{array}{r} {}^{5\ 10}\\ 8.6\cancel{0} \\ -\ 4.55 \\ \hline 5 \end{array}$$

STEP 3 Subtract the digits in the tenths place.

$$\begin{array}{r} {}^{5\ 10}\\ 8.6\cancel{0} \\ -\ 4.55 \\ \hline 05 \end{array}$$

STEP 4 Place the decimal point in the answer. Subtract the digits in the ones place.

$$\begin{array}{r} {}^{5\ 10}\\ 8.6\cancel{0} \\ -\ 4.55 \\ \hline 4.05 \end{array}$$

8.6 − 4.55 = 4.05

✓ Quick Check

Add or subtract.

1 4.59 + 1.02

2 9.04 − 6.32

3 5.8 + 0.26

Practice on Your Own
Add or subtract.

4 6.5 − 3.7

5 0.4 + 8.61

6 3.28 − 1.09

7 5.7 + 4.63

8 6.3 − 2.99

9 8.07 + 0.86

10 7.2 − 5.98

11 7.02 + 7.3

12 5.33 − 2.68

Express Improper Fractions as Mixed Numbers

TEACHING STRATEGY

1. **Vocabulary** Make sure students understand the terms *improper fraction* and *mixed number*. **Ask** Is $\frac{5}{6}$ a proper fraction or an improper fraction? Explain. [Possible answer: It is a proper fraction because the numerator is less than the denominator.] Why is $2\frac{3}{5}$ an example of a mixed number? [Possible answer: It is a number that combines a whole number and a fraction.]

2. **Teach** Work through the Example with students. Make sure that students understand how to rewrite the improper fraction in Step 1. **Ask** In Step 1, why is the numerator of $\frac{20}{6}$ written as the sum of 18 and 2? [Possible answer: You need to write the improper fraction as the sum of another improper fraction and a proper fraction. But the numerator of the improper fraction has to be divisible by the denominator. In the example, 6 is a factor of 18, so the numerator is divisible by the denominator.] In Step 3, how do you know that the fraction $\frac{2}{6}$ is not in simplest form? [The numerator and denominator can de divided by a common factor of 2.]

3. **Quick Check** Look for these common errors as students solve the Quick Check exercises.
   - Forgetting to reduce the fraction to simplest form before writing the mixed number.
   - Incorrectly breaking apart the numerator of the improper fraction, resulting in computation errors.

4. **Next Steps** Assign the practice exercises to students who show understanding. For students who need more support, provide tutoring using the alternate teaching strategy.

> ## Additional Teaching Resource
> 🖰 Online Transition Guide with Reteach and Extra Practice worksheets from previous grade levels

ALTERNATE INTERVENTION STRATEGY

Materials: none

Strategy: Use models to express improper fractions as mixed numbers.

1. Write $\frac{19}{4}$ on the board.

2. Draw a bar model to represent $\frac{19}{4}$. Point out that each bar is divided into fourths and explain that you need to draw enough bars in order to shade 19 parts. Point out to students that the shaded parts of the model represents $\frac{16}{4}$. **Ask** How many whole bars are shaded? [4] What fraction represents the last model? $\left[\frac{3}{4}\right]$

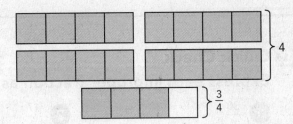

3. Have students combine the whole number and fraction to write the mixed number $4\frac{3}{4}$.

4. Using the same process, work through Example 1 on the student page, Before you have students combine the whole number and fraction, call their attention to the fraction $\frac{2}{6}$. Point out that $\frac{2}{6}$ is not in simplest form because the numerator and the denominator have a common factor, 2. Work with students to reduce the fraction to simplest form $\left(\frac{1}{3}\right)$ before writing the mixed number.

Express Improper Fractions as Mixed Numbers

Example

Express $\frac{20}{6}$ as a mixed number in simplest form.

STEP 1 Rewrite the improper fraction as a sum of an improper fraction and a proper fraction. The numerator of the improper fraction should be divisible by its denominator.

$$\frac{20}{6} = \frac{18+2}{6} = \frac{18}{6} + \frac{2}{6}$$

STEP 2 Write the improper fraction as a whole number.

$$\frac{18}{6} + \frac{2}{6} = 3 + \frac{2}{6}$$

STEP 3 Write the fraction in simplest form.

$$3 + \frac{2}{6} = 3 + \frac{1}{3}$$

STEP 4 Write the sum of the whole number and fraction as a mixed number.

$$3 + \frac{1}{3} = 3\frac{1}{3}$$

$\frac{20}{6}$ expressed as a mixed number in simplest form is $3\frac{1}{3}$.

✓ Quick Check

Express each improper fraction as a mixed number in simplest form.

1 $\frac{30}{4}$

2 $\frac{17}{2}$

3 $\frac{34}{5}$

_____   _____   _____

Practice on Your Own
Express each improper fraction as a mixed number in simplest form.

4 $\frac{29}{3}$

5 $\frac{34}{6}$

6 $\frac{18}{4}$

_____   _____   _____

7 $\frac{51}{7}$

8 $\frac{23}{5}$

9 $\frac{16}{3}$

_____   _____   _____

10 $\frac{74}{8}$

11 $\frac{43}{6}$

12 $\frac{57}{9}$

_____   _____   _____

Express Mixed Numbers as Improper Fractions

| TEACHING STRATEGY | ALTERNATE INTERVENTION STRATEGY |

TEACHING STRATEGY

1. **Vocabulary** Review the term *improper fraction* with students. How can you tell when a fraction is an improper fraction? [The numerator is greater than the denominator.] Then make sure students understand the terms used to name fractional parts, such as *thirds*, *fourths*, and *fifths*. **Ask** How many thirds equal 1 whole? [3] How many fourths equal 3 wholes? [12] How many fifths equal 2 wholes? [10]

2. **Teach** Work through the Example with students. Make sure that they understand how to rewrite the whole number as a fraction in Step 2. **Ask** How many fifths make 1 whole? [5] If $\frac{5}{5}$ make 1 whole, how many fifths make 3 wholes? [15] Students may need practice with renaming the whole number part of a mixed number as an equivalent number of ones and then renaming each one as an equivalent number of parts indicated by the denominator of the fraction part. For Step 4, remind students that when you add fractions with like denominators, you add the numerators and write their sum over the common denominator.

3. **Quick Check** Look for these common errors as students solve the Quick Check exercises.
   - Miscounting the number of wholes when writing them as fractions.
   - Adding the denominators of the fractions.
   - Mistakenly adding the denominator, the whole number, and the numerator in order to get the numerator for the improper fraction.

4. **Next Steps** Assign the practice exercises to students who show understanding. For students who need more support, provide tutoring using the alternate teaching strategy.

ALTERNATE INTERVENTION STRATEGY

Materials: none

Strategy: Use models to express mixed numbers as improper fractions.

1. Write $2\frac{3}{5}$ on the board.

2. Work with students to develop a model for the mixed number. Explain that the denominator in the fraction $\frac{3}{5}$ tells you that the model must be divided into fifths. **Ask** How many fifths make 1 whole? [5] On the board, draw one bar divided into fifths and shade all 5 parts. **Ask** How many wholes are in $2\frac{3}{5}$? [2] How many more models like this do I need to draw to show 2 wholes? [You need to draw 1 more model to represent 2.] Draw one last fifths bar and shade 3 of the parts to represent $\frac{3}{5}$.

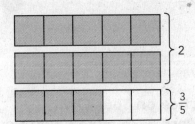

3. Have students examine the model. **Ask** How many fifths are shaded in all? [13 fifths are shaded.] Write this value as the improper fraction $\frac{13}{5}$ so that students can connect the model to the fraction.

4. Provide students with another mixed number. Have them work in pairs to model the number and then follow the same process to write an improper fraction based on their model.

Express Mixed Numbers as Improper Fractions

Example

Express $3\frac{2}{5}$ as an improper fraction.

STEP 1 Rewrite the mixed number as the sum of the whole number and the fraction.

$$3\frac{2}{5} = 3 + \frac{2}{5}$$

STEP 2 Write the whole number as a fraction. The denominator should be the same as the denominator of the fraction in the mixed number.

$$3 = \frac{5}{5} + \frac{5}{5} + \frac{5}{5} = \frac{15}{5}$$

STEP 3 Find the sum of the two fractions and express it as an improper fraction.

$$\frac{15}{5} + \frac{2}{5} = \frac{15+2}{5} = \frac{17}{5}$$

$3\frac{2}{5}$ expressed as an improper fraction is $\frac{17}{5}$.

✔ Quick Check

Express each mixed number as an improper fraction.

1 $2\frac{1}{2}$

2 $5\frac{2}{3}$

3 $6\frac{1}{4}$

Practice on Your Own

Express each mixed number as an improper fraction.

4 $4\frac{1}{9}$

5 $7\frac{3}{8}$

6 $1\frac{6}{7}$

7 $9\frac{5}{6}$

8 $6\frac{2}{3}$

9 $2\frac{4}{9}$

10 $4\frac{2}{7}$

11 $6\frac{3}{5}$

12 $8\frac{3}{4}$

Multiply Fractions by Fractions

TEACHING STRATEGY

1. **Vocabulary** Make sure students understand the terms *numerator, denominator,* and *common factor.* Write $\frac{6}{15}$ on the board. What number is the numerator? [6] The denominator? [15] What common factor can you use to simplify this fraction? [3]

2. **Teach** Remind students that the product of two fractions is equal to the product of the numerators over the product of the denominators. Work through the Examples with students. Then have students compare and contrast the two methods as a class. **Ask** What are some of the differences between the methods? [Possible answers: Method 1 involves fewer steps. Method 2 involves working with lesser numbers, and you do not have to write the fraction in simplest form as a last step.] Why do you end up with a fraction in simplest form in Method 2? [Possible answer: Because you have already divided the numerators and denominators by common factors before you multiply the two fractions.]

3. **Quick Check** Look for these common errors as students solve the Quick Check exercises.
   - Multiplying the numerators and writing the product over one of the denominators, which indicates confusion between multiplying fractions and adding fractions.
   - Incorrectly multiplying numerators or denominators.
   - Incorrectly choosing common factors or incorrectly dividing by common factors.

4. **Next Steps** Assign the practice exercises to students who show understanding. For students who need more support, provide tutoring using the alternate teaching strategy.

Additional Teaching Resource
🖲 Online Transition Guide with Reteach and Extra Practice worksheets from previous grade levels

ALTERNATE INTERVENTION STRATEGY

Materials: none

Strategy: Use rectangular arrays to model multiplication of fractions.

1. Tell students they are going to practice multiplying fractions using models. Write $\frac{3}{4} \cdot \frac{5}{7}$ on the board.

2. Instruct students to draw a rectangle and divide it into 4 rows of equal height. Explain that each row represents one-fourth. Have students shade 3 of the 4 rows to represent three-fourths.

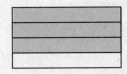

3. Next instruct students to divide the rectangle into 7 columns of equal width. **Ask** Why do you need 7 columns? [to represent sevenths] How many columns should you shade? [5] Encourage students to shade differently than before, such as using dots, diagonal lines, or a second color.

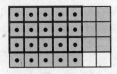

4. Explain to students that they have now modeled the product of $\frac{3}{4} \cdot \frac{5}{7}$. **Ask** How many of the parts have been shaded twice? [15] How many parts are there in the model in all? [28] On the board, write $\frac{3}{4} \cdot \frac{5}{7} = \frac{15}{28}$.

5. Have students repeat the exercise to find the products below. Remind them to simplify where appropriate.

$$\frac{5}{9} \cdot \frac{1}{4} \left[\frac{5}{36}\right] \qquad \frac{2}{5} \cdot \frac{3}{4} \left[\frac{3}{10}\right] \qquad \frac{4}{5} \cdot \frac{1}{6} \left[\frac{2}{15}\right]$$

Multiply Fractions by Fractions

Example 1 — Add Decimals

Find the product of $\frac{3}{8} \cdot \frac{2}{9}$.

STEP 1 Multiply the numerators.

$$\frac{3}{8} \cdot \frac{2}{9} = \frac{3 \cdot 2}{}$$

$$= \frac{6}{}$$

STEP 2 Multiply the denominators.

$$= \frac{6}{8 \cdot 9}$$

$$= \frac{6}{72}$$

STEP 3 Simplify the product. Divide the numerator and denominator by the common factor 6.

$$= \frac{6 \div 6}{72 \div 6}$$

$$= \frac{1}{12}$$

Example 2 — Subtract Decimals

Find the product of $\frac{3}{8} \cdot \frac{2}{9}$.

STEP 1 Divide by the common factor 2.

$$\frac{3}{8} \cdot \frac{2}{9} = \frac{3}{8 \div 2} \cdot \frac{2 \div 2}{9}$$

$$= \frac{3}{4} \cdot \frac{1}{9}$$

STEP 2 Divide by the common factor 3.

$$\frac{3}{4} \cdot \frac{1}{9} = \frac{3 \div 3}{4} \cdot \frac{1}{9 \div 3}$$

$$= \frac{1}{4} \cdot \frac{1}{3}$$

STEP 3 Multiply the numerators.

$$\frac{1}{4} \cdot \frac{1}{3} = \frac{1 \cdot 1}{}$$

$$= \frac{1}{}$$

STEP 4 Multiply the denominators.

$$= \frac{1}{4 \cdot 3}$$

$$= \frac{1}{12}$$

✔ Quick Check

Find each product in simplest form.

1 $\frac{3}{5} \cdot \frac{2}{3}$

2 $\frac{4}{9} \cdot \frac{3}{8}$

3 $\frac{4}{7} \cdot \frac{1}{6}$

Practice on Your Own
Find each product in simplest form.

4 $\frac{4}{5} \cdot \frac{5}{12}$

5 $\frac{2}{21} \cdot \frac{3}{8}$

6 $\frac{9}{14} \cdot \frac{2}{15}$

7 $\frac{5}{16} \cdot \frac{4}{30}$

8 $\frac{4}{5} \cdot \frac{25}{32}$

9 $\frac{3}{8} \cdot \frac{4}{21}$

Write Equivalent Fractions by Multiplication

TEACHING STRATEGY

1. **Vocabulary** Make sure students understand the term *equivalent*. Tell them that it means "equal in value" and that when they see the term, they can just think "equal." Remind students that the *numerator* is the top number in a fraction and that the *denominator*, the bottom number, is down below.

2. **Teach** Work through the Example with students. In Step 1, rewrite $\frac{5 \cdot 4}{6 \cdot 4}$ as $\frac{5}{6} \cdot \frac{4}{4}$. **Ask** When we multiply by $\frac{4}{4}$, what whole number are we multiplying by? [1] So, why does multiplying $\frac{5}{6}$ by $\frac{4}{4}$ produce a fraction equivalent to $\frac{5}{6}$? [Because when you multiply any number by 1, the result is equal to the original number.]

3. **Quick Check** Look for these common errors as students solve the Quick Check exercises.

   • Multiplying *only* the numerator or the denominator by another number.

   • Multiplying the numerator and denominator by different numbers.

   Both errors indicate a lack of understanding of the role of the Identity Property of Multiplication in writing equivalent fractions, that by multiplying the fraction by $\frac{a}{a}$ we are multiplying by 1, which results in a fraction that has the same value as the original fraction.

4. **Next Steps** Assign the practice exercises to students who show understanding. For students who need more support, provide tutoring using the alternate intervention strategy.

Additional Teaching Resource

Online Transition Guide with Reteach and Extra Practice worksheets from previous grade levels

ALTERNATE INTERVENTION STRATEGY

Materials: fraction models in halves, thirds, fourths, fifths, sixths, eighths, and tenths

Strategy: Use fraction models to identify equivalent fractions.

1. Distribute the fraction models. Write $\frac{1}{2}$. Direct students to select the fraction model that shows $\frac{1}{2}$. **Ask** How many equal parts is the fraction model divided into? [2] How many parts are shaded? [1]

2. Tell students to select the fourths fraction models, the ones that are divided into 4 equal parts. Have students align the four different fourths fraction model below the $\frac{1}{2}$ fraction model. **Ask** Looking at the shaded parts, which fourths fraction model is equivalent to $\frac{1}{2}$? [The one with 2 of the 4 equal parts shaded.]

$\frac{1}{2}$		$\frac{1}{2}$	$\frac{1}{2}$
$\frac{1}{4}$	$\frac{1}{4}$	$\frac{1}{4}$	$\frac{1}{4}$ $\frac{1}{4}$

3. Write $\frac{1}{2} = \frac{?}{4}$. Have students compare the shaded parts of the two models. **Ask** How many shaded parts in the fourths fraction model are equal to the shaded part in the halves fraction model? [2] So, what fraction is equivalent to $\frac{1}{2}$? $\left[\frac{2}{4}\right]$ Write $\frac{1}{2} = \frac{2}{4}$. Then demonstrate how students can find the same answer by multiplying both the numerator and denominator by 2.

4. Repeat this activity, using the models to identify other fractions equivalent to $\frac{1}{2}$. Demonstrate how to use multiplication to find each equivalent fraction.

Write Equivalent Fractions by Multiplication

Example

Express $\frac{5}{6}$ as two equivalent fractions using multiplication:

STEP 1 To write an equivalent fraction, multiply both the numerator and denominator of the fraction by the same number. This can be any whole number except 0 or 1.

$$\frac{5}{6} = \frac{5 \cdot 4}{6 \cdot 4} \quad \text{Multiply by 4.}$$
$$= \frac{20}{24}$$

STEP 2 To write a second equivalent fraction, repeat the process. Multiply both the numerator and denominator of the fraction by another number.

$$\frac{5}{6} = \frac{5 \cdot 9}{6 \cdot 9} \quad \text{Multiply by 9.}$$
$$= \frac{45}{54}$$

So, $\frac{5}{6}$, $\frac{20}{24}$, and $\frac{45}{54}$ are equivalent fractions. They all have the same value.

✓ Quick Check

Express each fraction as two equivalent fractions using multiplication.

1 $\frac{1}{2}$ 　　　　**2** $\frac{2}{3}$ 　　　　**3** $\frac{3}{8}$

_____   _____   _____

Practice on Your Own
Express each fraction as two equivalent fractions using multiplication.

4 $\frac{1}{4}$ 　　　　**5** $\frac{4}{5}$ 　　　　**6** $\frac{2}{7}$

_____   _____   _____

7 $\frac{8}{9}$ 　　　　**8** $\frac{5}{12}$ 　　　　**9** $\frac{3}{20}$

_____   _____   _____

Write Equivalent Fractions by Division

TEACHING STRATEGY

1. **Vocabulary** Make sure students understand the term *equivalent*. Tell them that it means "equal in value" and that when they see the term, they can just think "equal." Remind students that the *common factors* of two numbers are factors that they share.

2. **Teach** Work through the Example with students. In Step 1, rewrite $\frac{8 \div 2}{24 \div 2}$ as $\frac{8}{24} \div \frac{2}{2}$. **Ask** When we divide by $\frac{2}{2}$, what whole number are we dividing by? [1] So, why does dividing $\frac{8}{24}$ by $\frac{2}{2}$ produce a fraction equivalent to $\frac{8}{24}$? [Because when you divide any number by 1, the result is equal to the original number.]

3. **Quick Check** Look for these common errors as students solve the Quick Check exercises.
   - Dividing *only* the numerator or the denominator by another number.
   - Dividing the numerator and denominator by different numbers.
   Both errors indicate a lack of understanding of the role of the Identity Property of Division in writing equivalent fractions, that by dividing the fraction by $\frac{a}{a}$ we are dividing by 1, which results in a fraction that has the same value as the original fraction.

4. **Next Steps** Assign the practice exercises to students who show understanding. For students who need more support, provide tutoring using the alternate intervention strategy.

Additional Teaching Resource
Online Transition Guide with Reteach and Extra Practice worksheets from previous grade levels

ALTERNATE INTERVENTION STRATEGY

Materials: fraction models in halves, thirds, fourths, fifths, sixths, eighths, and tenths

Strategy: Use fraction models to identify equivalent fractions.

1. Distribute the fraction models. Write $\frac{4}{8}$. Direct students to select the fraction model that shows $\frac{4}{8}$. **Ask** How many equal parts is the fraction model divided into? [8] How many parts are shaded? [4]

2. Tell students to select the fourths fraction models, the ones that are divided into 4 equal parts. Have students align the four different fourths fraction models below the $\frac{4}{8}$ fraction model. **Ask** Looking at the shaded parts, which fourths fraction model is equivalent to $\frac{4}{8}$? [The one with 2 of the 4 equal parts shaded.]

$\frac{1}{4}$	$\frac{1}{4}$	$\frac{1}{4}$	$\frac{1}{4}$

$\frac{1}{8}$	$\frac{1}{8}$	$\frac{1}{8}$	$\frac{1}{8}$	$\frac{1}{8}$	$\frac{1}{8}$	$\frac{1}{8}$	$\frac{1}{8}$

3. Have students compare the shaded parts of the two models. **Ask** How many shaded parts in the fourths fraction model are equal to the shaded part in the halves fraction model? [2] So, what fraction is equivalent to $\frac{4}{8}$? $\left[\frac{2}{4}\right]$ Write $\frac{4}{8} = \frac{2}{4}$. Then demonstrate how students can find the same answer by dividing both the numerator and denominator by 2.

4. Repeat this activity, using the halves fraction models to identify another fraction equivalent to $\frac{4}{8}$. Demonstrate how to use division to find the equivalent fraction.

Write Equivalent Fractions by Division

Example

Express $\frac{8}{24}$ as two equivalent fractions using division.

STEP 1 Other than 1, identify common factors of both the numerator and denominator.

Factors of 8: 1, **2**, **4**, and **8**

Factors of 24: 1, **2**, 3, **4**, 6, **8**, 12, 24

STEP 2 Divide both the numerator and denominator of the fraction by one of the common factors.

$\frac{8}{24} = \frac{8 \div 2}{24 \div 2}$ Divide by 2.

$= \frac{4}{12}$

STEP 3 Divide both the numerator and denominator of the fraction by another common factor.

$\frac{8}{24} = \frac{8 \div 8}{24 \div 8}$ Divide by 8.

$= \frac{1}{3}$

So, $\frac{8}{24}$, $\frac{4}{12}$, and $\frac{1}{3}$ are equivalent fractions. They all have the same value.

✔ Quick Check

Express each fraction as two equivalent fractions using division.

1 $\frac{4}{36}$

2 $\frac{6}{12}$

3 $\frac{12}{20}$

Practice on Your Own
Express each fraction as two equivalent fractions using division.

4 $\frac{30}{42}$

5 $\frac{48}{72}$

6 $\frac{36}{56}$

7 $\frac{20}{68}$

8 $\frac{72}{132}$

9 $\frac{24}{156}$

Complete Equivalent Fractions

TEACHING STRATEGY	ALTERNATE INTERVENTION STRATEGY

TEACHING STRATEGY

1. **Vocabulary** Make sure students understand the term *equivalent*. **Ask** What does the term equivalent mean? [equal in value.] Remind students that the *numerator* is the top number in a fraction and that the *denominator*, the bottom number, is down below.

2. **Teach** Work through the examples with students. Have students look at the denominators in Example 1. **Ask** What was done to 5 to get 45? [It was multiplied by 9.] If 5 was multiplied by 9 to get 45, what must we do to 3 to find the missing numerator? [Multiply it by 9.] What is 3×9? [27] So, what fraction with a denominator of 45 is equivalent to $\frac{3}{5}$? $\left[\frac{27}{45}\right]$ Point out that we multiply $\frac{3}{5}$ by $\frac{9}{9}$. **Ask** When we multiply by $\frac{9}{9}$, it is the same as multiplying by what whole number? [1]

3. **Quick Check** Look for these common errors as students solve the Quick Check exercises.
   - Multiplying instead of dividing, or vice versa.
   - Multiplying (or dividing) the numerator and denominator by different numbers.

   Both errors indicate a lack of understanding that the same operation must be performed on both the numerator and denominator of the known fraction in order to produce an equivalent fraction.

4. **Next Steps** Assign the practice exercises to students who show understanding. For students who need more support, provide tutoring using the alternate intervention strategy.

Additional Teaching Resource

Online Transition Guide with Reteach and Extra Practice worksheets from previous grade levels

ALTERNATE INTERVENTION STRATEGY

Materials: none

Strategy: Use bar models to identify missing terms in equivalent fractions.

1. Write $\frac{2}{3} = \frac{?}{12}$. Below it draw two bar models shaded to show $\frac{2}{3}$.

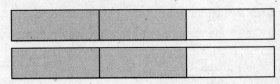

2. Tell students that in order to identify the missing term they need to divide the bottom bar model so that it shows twelfths instead of thirds. **Ask** To show twelfths, how many equal parts do we have to divide the bottom bar into? [12] Point out that the bar is now divided into 3 equal parts. **Ask** To divide the bar into 12 equal parts, how many pieces do we have to divide each of the parts into [4] Have a volunteer divide the second bar into equal twelfths.

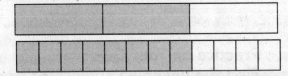

3. Have students compare the shaded parts of the two models. **Ask** How many shaded parts in the twelfths bar are equal to the shaded parts in the thirds bar? [8] So what is the missing numerator? [8] What fraction is equivalent to $\frac{2}{3}$? $\left[\frac{8}{12}\right]$ Demonstrate how students can find the same answer by multiplying both the numerator and denominator of the original fraction by 4.

4. Repeat this activity to identify the missing terms in $\frac{3}{4} = \frac{?}{16}$ and $\frac{2}{5} = \frac{8}{?}$. [12; 20] Demonstrate how to use multiplication to find the unknown term.

Complete Equivalent Fractions

Example 1 Unknown Numerator

Find the unknown numerator.

$$\frac{3}{5} = \frac{?}{45}$$

STEP 1 Both denominators are known.
Determine how the denominators,
5 and 45, are related to each other.

$$5 \times 9 = 45$$

STEP 2 Multiply both the numerator and
denominator of the original fraction by **9**.

$$\frac{3}{5} = \frac{3 \cdot 9}{5 \cdot 9}$$

$$= \frac{27}{45}$$

Example 2 Unknown Denominator

Find the unknown denominator.

$$\frac{2}{11} = \frac{14}{?}$$

STEP 1 Both numerators are known. Determine
how the numerators, 2 and 14, are
related to each other.

$$2 \times 7 = 14$$

STEP 1 Multiply both the numerator and
denominator of the original fraction by **7**.

$$\frac{2}{11} = \frac{2 \cdot 7}{11 \cdot 7}$$

$$= \frac{14}{77}$$

✔ Quick Check

Find the unknown numerator or denominator in each pair of equivalent fractions.

1 $\frac{4}{36} = \frac{?}{72}$

2 $\frac{4}{9} = \frac{28}{?}$

3 $\frac{7}{12} = \frac{?}{60}$

Practice on Your Own
Find the unknown numerator or denominator in each pair of equivalent fractions.

4 $\frac{9}{15} = \frac{36}{?}$

5 $\frac{3}{7} = \frac{?}{56}$

6 $\frac{8}{9} = \frac{72}{?}$

7 $\frac{3}{16} = \frac{?}{96}$

8 $\frac{12}{?} = \frac{84}{105}$

9 $\frac{?}{14} = \frac{25}{70}$

10 $\frac{5}{12} = \frac{65}{?}$

11 $\frac{?}{18} = \frac{18}{108}$

12 $\frac{6}{?} = \frac{78}{143}$

Write Fractions in Simplest Form

TEACHING STRATEGY

1. **Vocabulary** Review the meaning of *simplest form*. Write $\frac{2}{3}$. **Ask** What are the factors of the numerator 2? [1 and 2] What are the factors of the denominator 3? [1 and 3] How many factors do 2 and 3 share? [one] What is the common factor? [1] Why is $\frac{2}{3}$ in simplest form? [The only common factor of the numerator and denominator is 1.]

2. **Teach** Review how to find the factors of a number and how to identify the greatest common factor of two numbers. **Ask** What are the factors of 8? [1, 2, 4, and 8] What are the factors of 12? [1, 2, 3, 4, 6, and 12] What is the greatest common factor of 8 and 12? [4] Then work through the example with students. **Ask** What would happen if you divided the numerator and denominator of $\frac{18}{45}$ by 3? [Possible answer: You would simplify the fraction to $\frac{6}{15}$, but this is not in simplest form. 6 and 15 have a common factor of 3.]

3. **Quick Check** Look for these common errors as students solve the Quick Check exercises.
   - Choosing a common factor that is not the greatest common factor, yielding an answer that is an equivalent fraction but is not in *simplest* form.
   - Dividing the numerator by one factor and the denominator by a different factor.

   These errors indicate a lack of understanding that the *greatest common* factor must be used to reduce a fraction to simplest form.

4. **Next Steps** Assign the practice exercises to students who show understanding. For students who need more support, provide tutoring using the alternate teaching strategy.

Additional Teaching Resource

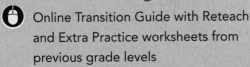 Online Transition Guide with Reteach and Extra Practice worksheets from previous grade levels

ALTERNATE INTERVENTION STRATEGY

Materials: none

Strategy: Use repeated division by common factors to write a fraction in simplest form.

1. Tell students that it is not necessary to divide by the greatest common factor of the numerator and denominator to rewrite a fraction in simplest form. They can also use repeated division by other common factors.

2. Write $\frac{36}{54}$ on the board. **Ask** Besides 1, what is a common factor of both the numerator 36 and the denominator 54? [Possible answer: 2] What is 36 divided by 2? [18] What is 54 divided by 2? [27]

3. Write $\frac{36}{54} = \frac{36 \div 2}{54 \div 2} = \frac{18}{27}$ on the board. **Ask** Is $\frac{18}{27}$ in simplest form? [No.] **Ask** Besides 1, what is a common factor of both the numerator 18 and the denominator 27? [Possible answer: 3] What is 18 divided by 3? [6] What is 27 divided by 3? [9]

4. Write $\frac{18}{27} = \frac{18 \div 3}{27 \div 3} = \frac{6}{9}$ on the board. **Ask** Is $\frac{6}{9}$ in simplest form? [No.] **Ask** Besides 1, what is a common factor of both the numerator 6 and the denominator 9? [3] What is 6 divided by 3? [2] What is 9 divided by 3? [3]

5. Write $\frac{6}{9} = \frac{6 \div 3}{9 \div 3} = \frac{2}{3}$ on the board. **Ask** Is $\frac{2}{3}$ in simplest form? [Yes.] How do you know $\frac{2}{3}$ is in simplest form? [The only common factor of the numerator and denominator is 1.]

6. Repeat the activity to find the simplest form of $\frac{48}{84}$ and $\frac{72}{144}$. $\left[\frac{4}{7} \text{ and } \frac{1}{2}\right]$

Write Fractions in Simplest Form

Name _____ Date _____

Example

Write $\frac{18}{45}$ in simplest form.

STEP 1 List all the factors of the numerator and all the factors of the denominator.

numerator →   18   1, 2, 3, 6, 9, 18
denominator →   45   1, 3, 5, 9, 15, 45

STEP 2 Identify common factors.

numerator →   18   **1**, 2, **3**, 6, **9**, 18
denominator →   45   **1**, **3**, 5, **9**, 15, 45

STEP 3 Identify the greatest common factor.
The greatest common factor of 18 and 45 is 9.

STEP 4 Divide both the numerator and the denominator by the greatest common factor.

$$\frac{18}{45} = \frac{18 \div 9}{45 \div 9} = \frac{2}{5}$$

$\frac{18}{45}$ written in simplest form is $\frac{2}{5}$.

☑ Quick Check

Write each fraction in simplest form.

1 $\frac{14}{49}$ _____

2 $\frac{16}{24}$ _____

3 $\frac{8}{32}$ _____

4 $\frac{6}{20}$ _____

5 $\frac{15}{35}$ _____

6 $\frac{4}{12}$ _____

Practice on Your Own
Write each fraction in simplest form.

7 $\frac{36}{63}$ _____

8 $\frac{8}{40}$ _____

9 $\frac{25}{35}$ _____

10 $\frac{48}{54}$ _____

11 $\frac{9}{12}$ _____

12 $\frac{12}{36}$ _____

13 $\frac{35}{42}$ _____

14 $\frac{40}{90}$ _____

15 $\frac{10}{16}$ _____

16 $\frac{11}{110}$ _____

17 $\frac{18}{81}$ _____

18 $\frac{24}{80}$ _____

Convert Measurements

TEACHING STRATEGY

1. **Vocabulary** Review the unit names and abbreviations for the customary and metric systems. Then review the definition for the term *conversion factor* with students. **Ask** How many inches are equal to 1 foot? [12 inches]

2. **Teach** Begin by making sure that students have a good understanding of the relative sizes of the different units of measure. You may wish to display two tables of conversion factors for length, capacity, and weight/mass: one for customary units and another for metric units. **Ask** When converting from a larger unit, such as meters, to a smaller unit, such as centimeters, will the answer have more units or fewer units? [The answer will have more units.] What operation should you use to get an answer with more units? [multiplication] When converting from a smaller unit, such as inches, to a larger unit, such as feet, will the answer have more units or fewer units? [The answer will have fewer units.] What operation should you use to get an answer with fewer units? [division] Work through the examples with students.

3. **Quick Check** Look for these common errors as students solve the Quick Check exercises.
   - Multiplying when they should divide and dividing when they should multiply, indicating a lack of awareness of the relative size of the two units involved.
   - Confusing the conversion factors used to convert from one unit to another.

4. **Next Steps** Assign the practice exercises to students who show understanding. For students who need more support, provide tutoring using the alternate teaching strategy.

Additional Teaching Resource
 Online Transition Guide with Reteach and Extra Practice worksheets from previous grade levels

ALTERNATE INTERVENTION STRATEGY

Materials: inch cubes, customary rulers, yardsticks, centimeter cubes, metric rulers, meter sticks

Strategy: Use models to convert units of measure.

1. You may wish to have two sessions for this activity, treating the customary and metric systems separately.

2. Have students gather around a table to examine the inch cubes, ruler, and yardstick.

3. Display 12 inch-cubes. Have students verify that 1 cube is 1 inch long. Display the inch ruler. Students should note that it takes 12 cubes or 12 inches to equal 1 ruler or 1 foot. **Ask** How many feet are equal to 12 inches? [1 foot] How can you find the number of feet in 36 inches? [Possible answer: 12 + 12 + 12 = 36, so 36 inches is equal to 3 feet.] Explain that when converting a smaller unit to a larger unit, the result will be fewer units. So, the operation to use is division: 36 ÷ 12 = 3. Model the same process for converting from yards to feet.

4. Then reverse the process, converting from feet to inches. Explain that when converting a larger unit to a smaller unit, the result will be more units. So, the operation to use is multiplication. **Ask** How can you find the number of inches in 2 feet? [Possible answer: If there are 12 inches in 1 foot, then there are 12 + 12, or 24 inches, in 2 feet.] Help students see that you can multiply the number of feet by the number of inches in 1 foot to find the number of inches in 2 feet: 2 · 12 = 24. Model the same process for converting from feet to yards.

5. As you model the same process for the metric system, help students understand that the same operations—multiplication and division—are used to convert between metric units.

Convert Measurements

Name _____ Date _____

Example 1 Customary Units

Find the unknown measurement.

$$9 \text{ ft} = ? \text{ yd}$$

STEP 1 Identify the conversion factor for feet and yards.

$$1 \text{ yd} = 3 \text{ ft}$$

STEP 2 To convert from a smaller unit (ft) to a larger unit (yd), divide. Divide the number of feet by the number of feet in 1 yard.

$$9 \div 3 = 3$$

So, 9 ft = 3 yd.

Example 2 Metric Units

Find the unknown measurement.

$$25 \text{ m} = ? \text{ cm}$$

STEP 1 Identify the conversion factor for centimeters and meters.

$$1 \text{ m} = 100 \text{ cm}$$

STEP 1 To convert from a larger unit (m) to a smaller unit (cm), multiply. Multiply the number of meters by the number of centimeters in 1 meter.

$$25 \cdot 100 = 2,500$$

So, 25 m = 2,500 cm.

☑ Quick Check

Find the unknown measurement.

1 2 lb = __?__ oz

2 0.01 L = __?__ mL

3 72 in. = __?__ yd

Practice on Your Own
Find the unknown measurement.

4 4 gal = __?__ qt

5 1,500 mg = __?__ g

6 8 ft = __?__ in.

7 0.2 kg = __?__ g

8 6 c = __?__ pt

9 450 mm = __?__ m

10 960 yd = __?__ ft

11 80 oz = __?__ lb

12 5.5 km = __?__ m

Interpret a Comparison Bar Model

TEACHING STRATEGY

1. **Vocabulary** Make sure students understand the term *unit* as it relates to comparison bar models and the unitary method. **Ask** When we use the term *unit* to compare lengths of bar models, what part of the model are we talking about? [a single part, or section, of the bar] In the pairs of bar models we are using here, what is true about all the parts of both bars? [All the parts are the same size.]

2. **Teach** Tell students that the strategy they are using here to identify the unknown quantities in each pair of bar models is known as the *unitary method*. Explain that when we use this method, we first find the value of a single part, or unit, of the bars. Then we can use that value to calculate the value of each bar, the value of the difference in their lengths, or the sum of the lengths of both bars.

   Work through the examples with students. Direct students to the model in Example 1. Point out the two brackets labeled "?". **Ask** What values are unknown in this model? [the length of Bar A and the length of Bar B] Point out the bracket labeled "20" along the top of the model. **Ask** What does this label refer to? [the difference in lengths between the two bars] How many units, or parts of a bar, does the bracket labeled "20" span? [It spans 4 units, or parts, of the bottom bar.]

   Direct students to the first computation line in Step 1. **Ask** If the value of four units is 20, what is the value of one unit? [5] Direct students to Step 2. **Ask** How many units are in

   Bar A? [2] If the value of each unit is 5, what is the value of Bar A? [10] **Ask** How many units, or parts, are in Bar B? [6] If the value of each unit is 5, what is the value of Bar A? [30].

   Direct students to the model in Example 2. Point out the two brackets labeled "?". **Ask** What values are unknown in this model? [the length of Bar A and the length of Bar B] Point out the bracket labeled "88" at the right side of the model. **Ask** What does this label refer to? [the sum of the lengths of Bar A and Bar B] How many total units, or parts of a bar, are there in Bar A and Bar B together? [11 units]

   Direct students to the first computation line in Step 1. **Ask** If the value of 11 units is 88, what is the value of one unit? [8] Direct students to Step 2. **Ask** How many units, or parts, are in Bar A? [7] If the value of each unit is 8, what is the value of Bar A? [56] **Ask** How many units, or parts, are in Bar B? [4] If the value of each unit is 8, what is the value of Bar A? [32]

3. **Quick Check** Look for these common errors as students solve the Quick Check exercises.
   - When the given value refers to the difference in the length of the two bars, dividing that value by the total number of units in the model rather than the number of units in the difference.
   - When the given value refers to the total length of the two bars, dividing that value by the number of units that represents the difference in bar lengths rather than the number of units in both bars.

4. **Next Steps** Assign the practice exercises to students who show understanding.

Additional Teaching Resource
🖱 Online Transition Guide with Reteach and Extra Practice worksheets from previous grade levels

Interpret a Comparison Bar Model

Example 1 **Given the difference**

Find the value of A and B.

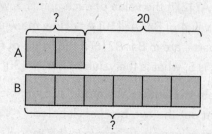

STEP 1 The difference between the two bars, 20, is equal to 4 units of a bar. Divide to find the value of a single unit of the bars.

4 units → 20

1 unit → $\frac{20}{4}$ = **5**

STEP 2 Count the number of units in each bar. Multiply each number of units by **5**.

Value of A: 2 units → 2 × 5 = 10
Value of B: 6 units → 6 → 5 = 30

Example 2 **Given the sum**

Find the value of A and B.

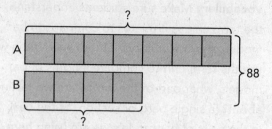

STEP 1 The sum of the two bars, 88, is equal to 11 units of the bars. Divide to find the value of a single unit of the bars.

11 units → 88

1 unit → $\frac{88}{11}$ = **8**

STEP 2 Count the number of units in each bar. Multiply each number of units by **8**.

Value of A: 7 units → 7 × 8 = 56
Value of B: 4 units → 4 × 8 = 32

✔ Quick Check

Find the values of P and Q.

1
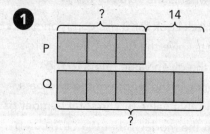

_____

2
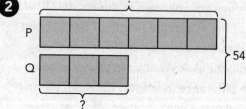

_____

Practice on Your Own
Find the values of P and Q.

3
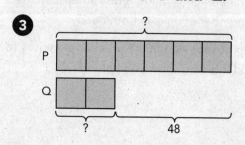

_____

4
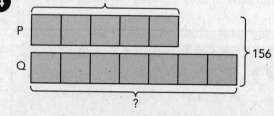

_____

Multiply Whole Numbers

TEACHING STRATEGY

1. **Vocabulary** Review the names of terms in a multiplication problem. Using the worksheet, have students identify examples of the following terms: *factor, partial product, and product.*

2. **Teach** Work through the examples with students. For Example 1, remind them when multiplying by the tens digit to first place a zero in the ones column at left as a place holder. **Ask** Why do you need to place the zero when multiplying by the tens digit, 4? [Possible answer: You are multiplying 37 by 40, which is 1,480. So you need to place the 0 to make sure the digits are in the correct place. If you didn't place the 0, you would be finding the product of $37 \cdot 4$, not 40.] When do you add in the regrouped 5 and 2? [After you multiply $8 \cdot 3$ and after you multiply $4 \cdot 3$] In Example 2, remind students to place two zeros—one in the ones column and one in the tens column—when multiplying by the hundreds digit, 2 **Ask** When do you add the regrouped 4, 3, 3, 2, and 1? [after multiplying $8 \cdot 4$, $8 \cdot 3$, $5 \cdot 4$, $5 \cdot 3$, and $4 \cdot 2$]

3. **Quick Check** Look for these common errors as students solve the Quick Check exercises.
   - Forgetting to place zeros at right when multiplying by the tens or hundreds, indicating a lack of attention to place value.
   - Forgetting to add the regrouped numbers after multiplying, indicating confusion about the algorithm for multiplication.

4. **Next Steps** Assign the practice exercises to students who show understanding. For students who need more support, provide tutoring using the alternate teaching strategy.

Additional Teaching Resource
Online Transition Guide with Reteach and Extra Practice worksheets from previous grade levels

ALTERNATE INTERVENTION STRATEGY

Materials: none

Strategy: To multiply whole numbers, break apart one of the factors into expanded form.

1. Work with students to find the product of $456 \cdot 237$ by following the steps below.

2. Break apart 237 into expanded form.

   $237 = 200 + 30 + 7$

3. Multiply 456 by each number.

   $456 \cdot 200 = 91,200$
   $456 \cdot 30 = 13,680$
   $456 \cdot 7 = 3,192$

4. Add the products.

$$
\begin{array}{r}
91,200 \\
13,680 \\
+3,192 \\
\hline
108,072
\end{array}
$$

5. Relate the products found using this method to the partial products in the traditional algorithm.

$$
\begin{array}{r}
456 \\
\times 237 \\
\hline
\end{array}
$$

3,192	$456 \cdot 7 = 3,192$
13,680	$456 \cdot 30 = 13,680$
91,200	$456 \cdot 200 = 91,200$
108,072	

6. Work through other similar exercises with students. Be sure to include numbers with 0 in the ones or tens place.

Multiply Whole Numbers

Example 1	**Two-Digit Numbers**

Find 48 · 37.

$$
\begin{array}{r}
{\scriptstyle 2} \\
{\scriptstyle 5} \\
37 \\
\times \quad 48 \\
\hline
296 \\
1{,}480 \\
\hline
1{,}776
\end{array}
$$

296   Multiply 37 by 8 ones.

1,480   Multiply 37 by 4 tens, or 40.

1,776   Add the products.

Example 2	**Three-Digit Numbers**

Find 258 · 346.

$$
\begin{array}{r}
{\scriptstyle 1} \\
{\scriptstyle 2\,3} \\
{\scriptstyle 3\,4} \\
346 \\
\times \quad 258 \\
\hline
2{,}768 \\
17{,}300 \\
69{,}200 \\
\hline
89{,}268
\end{array}
$$

2,768   Multiply 346 by 8 ones.

17,300   Multiply 346 by 5 tens, or 50.

69,200   Multiply 346 by 2 hundreds, or 200.

89,268   Add the products.

✔ Quick Check

Find the product.

1 49 · 61

2 355 · 27

3 242 · 368

Practice on Your Own

Find the product.

4 193 · 22

5 47 · 95

6 501 · 374

7 813 · 450

8 544 · 872

9 392 · 27

10 471 · 511

11 29 · 318

12 514 · 293

13 80 · 52

14 703 · 35

15 189 · 325

Multiply Fractions by Whole Numbers

TEACHING STRATEGY

1. **Vocabulary** Make sure students understand the following terms: *numerator*, *denominator*, *simplest form*, and *common factor*. Using the worksheet, have volunteers identify examples of each term.

2. **Teach** Work through Example 1 with students. Be sure students understand that you must divide both the denominator, 4, and the whole number, 8, by the common factor 2. Explain that you also could divide by the common factor 4: $\frac{3}{4} \cdot 8 = \frac{3}{4 \div 4} \cdot (8 \div 4) = \frac{3}{1} \cdot 2 = 3 \cdot 2 = 6$. Then work through Example 2 with students. **Ask** Why is the first step in Example 2 different from the first step in Example 1? [Possible answer: There is no common factor for 7 and 5, so you cannot divide by a common factor as a first step.] How can the improper fraction $\frac{10}{7}$ be written as $1\frac{3}{7}$? [Divide 10 by 7, which is 1 R3. Write the whole number 1, write the remainder as the numerator, and 7 as the denominator to get $1\frac{3}{7}$.]

3. **Quick Check** Look for these common errors as students solve the Quick Check exercises.
   - Leaving the product as an improper fraction rather than writing it as a mixed number.
   - Forgetting to divide by a common factor, when possible. This poses a problem only if students make mathematical errors as a result of having to work with larger numbers.

4. **Next Steps** Assign the practice exercises to students who show understanding. For students who need more support, provide tutoring using the alternate teaching strategy.

Additional Teaching Resource

🖱 Online Transition Guide with Reteach and Extra Practice worksheets from previous grade levels

ALTERNATE INTERVENTION STRATEGY

Materials: TRT12 (Grid Paper)

Strategy: Use bars to model how to find the product of a fraction and a whole number.

1. Write $\frac{2}{5} \cdot 3$ on the board.

2. Draw a bar divided into equal fifths. Shade 2 of the parts to model $\frac{2}{5}$.

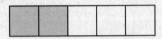

3. Now shade 3 times the amount shown in the model. Note that you will need another bar to do this. **Ask** What fraction does this model show? [The model shows $\frac{6}{5}$ or $1\frac{1}{5}$.]

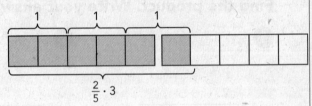

$$\frac{2}{5} \cdot 3$$

So, $\frac{2}{5} \cdot 3 = \frac{6}{5} = 1\frac{1}{5}$.

4. Work through other examples with students. Try some examples where the answer is a fraction or whole number: $\frac{2}{7} \cdot 3$ and $\frac{5}{6} \cdot 12$.

5. As students become familiar with the model, connect the drawings to the method of multiplying a fraction by a whole number shown in Examples 1 and 2.

Multiply Fractions by Whole Numbers

Name _____ Date _____

Example 1

Find $\frac{3}{4} \cdot 8$.

$\frac{3}{4} \cdot 8 = \frac{3}{4 \div 2} \cdot (8 \div 2) = \frac{3}{2} \cdot 4$ Divide the denominator and the whole number by the common factor 2.

$= \frac{3 \cdot 4}{2} = \frac{12}{2}$ Multiply the numerator by the whole number.

$= 6$ Write the product in simplest form.

Example 2

Find $\frac{2}{7} \cdot 5$.

$\frac{2}{7} \cdot 5 = \frac{2 \cdot 5}{7} = \frac{10}{7}$ Since there is no common factor for 7 and 5, multiply the numerator by the whole number.

$= 1\frac{3}{7}$ Write the product in simplest form.

Quick Check

Find the product. Write your answer in simplest form.

1 $\frac{2}{5} \cdot 3$

2 $\frac{3}{4} \cdot 4$

3 $\frac{7}{8} \cdot 6$

_____   _____   _____

Practice on Your Own

Find the product. Write your answer in simplest form.

4 $\frac{2}{3} \cdot 9$

5 $4 \cdot \frac{3}{5}$

6 $\frac{2}{5} \cdot 15$

_____   _____   _____

7 $\frac{3}{10} \cdot 2$

8 $\frac{5}{8} \cdot 4$

9 $\frac{5}{12} \cdot 2$

_____   _____   _____

10 $\frac{2}{21} \cdot 7$

11 $9 \cdot \frac{5}{6}$

12 $\frac{1}{3} \cdot 6$

_____   _____   _____

Multiply Mixed Numbers and Whole Numbers

TEACHING STRATEGY	ALTERNATE INTERVENTION STRATEGY

TEACHING STRATEGY

1. **Vocabulary** Make sure students understand the following terms: *mixed number* and *improper fraction*. Using the worksheet, have volunteers identify examples of each term.

2. **Teach** Work through the Example with students. Review how to write a mixed number as an improper fraction: $a\dfrac{b}{c} = \dfrac{(a \cdot c) + b}{c}$. Make sure students understand that you must multiply the denominator by the whole number before adding the numerator. **Ask** When writing a mixed number as an improper fraction, what would happen if you added the numerator and denominator, and then multiplied by the whole number? Explain. [Possible answer: The improper fraction would not have the same value as the mixed number.] Draw students' attention to Step 3.

   Ask Why is it helpful to divide the denominator and whole number by the common factor 2? [Possible answer: The product will not have to be simplified as much—or at all—if you divide by a common factor before you multiply.]

3. **Quick Check** Look for these common errors as students solve the Quick Check exercises.
   - Incorrectly writing a mixed number as an improper fraction by multiplying and adding in the wrong order.
   - Neglecting to write the answer in simplest form.

4. **Next Steps** Assign the practice exercises to students who show understanding. For students who need more support, provide tutoring using the alternate teaching strategy.

Additional Teaching Resource
Online Transition Guide with Reteach and Extra Practice worksheets from previous grade levels

ALTERNATE INTERVENTION STRATEGY

Materials: TRT12 (Grid Paper)

Strategy: Use models to represent finding the product of a whole number and a mixed number.

1. Write $2\dfrac{2}{3} \cdot 5$ on the board.

2. Draw a bar model to represent $2\dfrac{2}{3}$. **Ask** How does this model show $2\dfrac{2}{3}$? [Possible answer: Two bars are fully shaded, which represents the whole number 2. In the third bar, 2 out of 3 parts are shaded, which represents the fraction $\dfrac{2}{3}$.]

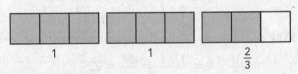

$$1 \qquad\qquad 1 \qquad\qquad \tfrac{2}{3}$$

3. Repeat the model 5 times to show $2\dfrac{2}{3} \cdot 5$.

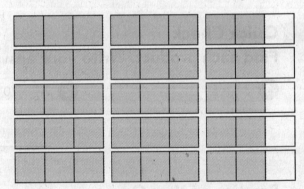

3. Work with students to quantify the product. **Ask** How many bars are fully shaded? [10] Direct students to the five partially shaded bars in the third column. **Ask** What is $\dfrac{10}{3}$ written as a mixed number? $\left[3\dfrac{1}{3}\right]$ What is $10 + 3\dfrac{1}{3}$? $\left[13\dfrac{1}{3}\right]$. So, $2\dfrac{2}{3} \cdot 5 = 13\dfrac{1}{3}$.

4. As students become more comfortable with using models, you may want them to break apart the mixed number and multiply the parts without the models.

Multiply Mixed Numbers and Whole Numbers

Example

Find $2\frac{5}{6} \cdot 8$.

STEP 1 Rewrite the mixed number as an improper fraction.

$$2\frac{5}{6} = \frac{17}{6}$$

STEP 2 In the original expression, replace the mixed number with the improper fraction.

$$2\frac{5}{6} \cdot 8 = \frac{17}{6} \cdot 8$$

STEP 3 If possible, divide the denominator and whole number by a common factor.
In this example, divide both by the common factor 2.

$$\frac{17}{6} \cdot 8 = \frac{17}{6 \div 2} \cdot (8 \div 2) = \frac{17}{3} \cdot 4$$

STEP 4 Multiply. Write the product in simplest form.

$$\frac{17}{3} \cdot 4 = \frac{17 \cdot 4}{3} = \frac{68}{3} = 22\frac{2}{3}$$

✓ Quick Check

Find each product. Write your answer in simplest form.

1 $3\frac{1}{4} \cdot 5$

2 $2\frac{2}{5} \cdot 10$

3 $4\frac{2}{7} \cdot 3$

_____   _____   _____

Practice on Your Own

Find each product. Write your answer in simplest form.

4 $6 \cdot 2\frac{1}{4}$

5 $3\frac{3}{8} \cdot 4$

6 $3\frac{1}{6} \cdot 2$

_____   _____   _____

7 $5 \cdot 2\frac{2}{5}$

8 $4\frac{3}{7} \cdot 2$

9 $1\frac{2}{5} \cdot 3$

_____   _____   _____

Divide With Fractions and Whole Numbers

TEACHING STRATEGY

1. **Vocabulary** Make sure students understand the term *reciprocal*. **Ask** What is the reciprocal of 16? $\left[\frac{1}{16}\right]$ What is the reciprocal of $\frac{5}{8}$? $\left[\frac{8}{5}\right]$ Remind them that a reciprocal is one of two numbers whose product is 1.

2. **Teach** Work through the examples with students. Point out that dividing by a number is the same as multiplying by the number's reciprocal. **Ask** For Example 1, what number multiplied by 12 is equal to 1? $\left[\frac{1}{12}\right]$ For Example 2, what number multiplied by $\frac{2}{5}$ is equal to 1? $\left[\frac{5}{2}\right]$ Make sure students understand how the quotient in each example compares to the dividend. **Ask** When you divide a fraction less than 1 by a whole number, how does the quotient compare in value to the dividend? [The quotient is always less than the original fraction.] When you divide a whole number by a fraction less than 1, how does the quotient compare to the dividend? [The quotient is always greater than the dividend.]

3. **Quick Check** Look for these common errors as students solve the Quick Check exercises.
   - Forgetting to rewrite the expression using the reciprocal of the divisor.
   - Incorrectly inverting the dividend or the quotient rather than the divisor.
   Both of these errors indicate confusion about the algorithm.

4. **Next Steps** Assign the practice exercises to students who show understanding. For students who need more support, provide tutoring using the alternate teaching strategy.

Additional Teaching Resource

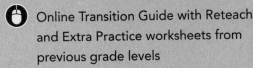 Online Transition Guide with Reteach and Extra Practice worksheets from previous grade levels

ALTERNATE INTERVENTION STRATEGY

Materials: none

Strategy: Divide with fractions and whole numbers without finding common factors before multiplying. This gives the correct answer, but requires students to work with larger numbers.

1. Write $15 \div \frac{5}{6}$ on the board.

2. Rewrite the expression as a multiplication expression using the reciprocal of the divisor.
$$15 \div \frac{5}{6} = 15 \cdot \frac{6}{5}$$

3. Multiply the whole number 15 and the numerator 6. Write the product over the denominator 5.
$$15 \cdot \frac{6}{5} = \frac{15 \cdot 6}{5} = \frac{90}{5}$$

4. Simplify the product.
$$\frac{90}{5} = 18$$

5. Work through other examples with students. Use examples where the whole number and numerator have a common factor (e.g., $\frac{4}{5} \div 12$). Do not divide any terms by the common factor before multiplying.

6. After students are comfortable with this method, show them how finding a common factor before multiplying can make the computation easier.

$$15 \div \frac{5}{6} \qquad\qquad \frac{4}{5} \div 12$$
$$15 \div \frac{5}{6} = 15 \cdot \frac{6}{5} \qquad \frac{4}{5} \div 12 = \frac{4}{5} \cdot \frac{1}{12}$$
$$= 3 \cdot 6 \qquad\qquad = \frac{1}{5} \cdot \frac{1}{3}$$
$$= 18 \qquad\qquad\quad = \frac{1}{15}$$

Divide With Fractions and Whole Numbers

Name _____ **Date** _____

Example 1 Fraction by Whole Numbers

Find $\frac{2}{3} \div 12$.

$\frac{2}{3} \div 12 = \frac{2}{3} \cdot \frac{1}{12}$ Rewrite as a multiplication expression using the reciprocal of the divisor.

$= \frac{2 \div 2}{3} \cdot \frac{1}{12 \div 2}$ Divide the numerator 2 and the denominator 12 by the common factor 2.

$= \frac{1}{3} \cdot \frac{1}{6}$

$= \frac{1}{18}$ Multiply.

Example 2 Whole Numbers by Fraction

Find $14 \div \frac{2}{5}$.

$14 \div \frac{2}{5} = 14 \cdot \frac{5}{2}$ Rewrite as a multiplication expression using the reciprocal of the divisor.

$= (14 \div 2) \cdot \frac{5}{2 \div 2}$ Divide the whole number and the denominator by the common factor 2.

$= 7 \cdot 5$

$= 35$ Multiply.

✔ Quick Check
Find each quotient. Write your answer in simplest form.

1 $\frac{3}{4} \div 6$

2 $7 \div \frac{3}{8}$

3 $\frac{7}{8} \div 3$

Practice on Your Own
Find each quotient. Write your answer in simplest form.

4 $\frac{3}{4} \div 5$

5 $5 \div \frac{3}{4}$

6 $16 \div \frac{1}{8}$

7 $11 \div \frac{3}{7}$

8 $9 \div \frac{5}{6}$

9 $10 \div \frac{2}{3}$

Divide Fractions

TEACHING STRATEGY

1. **Vocabulary** Using the worksheet, have students identify examples of these terms: *reciprocal*, *mixed number*, and *common factor*.

2. **Teach** Work through the examples with students. In Example 1, remind students that they must find the reciprocal of the divisor. **Ask** Which number is the divisor? $\left[\frac{3}{8}\right]$ What is the reciprocal of $\frac{3}{8}$? $\left[\frac{3}{8}\right]$ In Example 2, point out that the order in which you divide by common factors does not matter. However, explain that it is best to use the greatest common factor because it will result in fewer steps and make it easier to compute. Draw students' attention to the third step in Example 2. **Ask** What would happen if you divided by 5 instead of 15? [You would have the numerator 3 and the denominator 6, but they still have a common factor of 3. So you would need to divide by the common factor again.] Why is it a good practice to divide by common factors before you multiply? [Possible answer: When you divide by common factors, the remaining numbers are easier to compute with.]

3. **Quick Check** Look for these common errors as students solve the Quick Check exercises.
   - Finding the reciprocal of the dividend, not the divisor.
   - Forgetting to write any improper fractions as mixed numbers in their answers.

4. **Next Steps** Assign the practice exercises to students who show understanding. For students who need more support, provide tutoring using the alternate teaching strategy.

Additional Teaching Resource
Online Transition Guide with Reteach and Extra Practice worksheets from previous grade levels

ALTERNATE INTERVENTION STRATEGY

Materials: TRT12 (Grid Paper), 2 colored pencils

Strategy: Use models to represent dividing fractions.

1. Explain to students that dividing fractions involves the same steps as dividing whole numbers and fractions. Write $6 \div \frac{1}{2} = 12$ on the board. **Ask** Compare the values of the quotient and the dividend. What do you notice? [The quotient is twice the value of the dividend.]

2. Write $\frac{3}{4} \div \frac{1}{2}$ on the board. **Ask** Based on what we just observed, what do you think the quotient is? $\left[\frac{3}{4} \cdot 2, \text{ or } 1\frac{1}{2}\right]$ Model the problem for students by drawing a bar to show $\frac{3}{4}$. Then divide the model in half. Point out that the model now shows 1 whole and $\frac{1}{2}$, or $1\frac{1}{2}$.

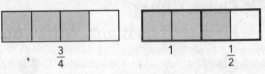

3. Repeat the process to model $\frac{1}{2} \div \frac{1}{4}$.

4. Once students are comfortable with modeling division with fractions, connect the model for $\frac{3}{4} \div \frac{1}{2}$ to the algorithm. Remind students that multiplication and division are inverse operations. Dividing by $\frac{1}{2}$ is the same as multiplying by 2. Because you are using an inverse operation, you need to use the "inverse" of $\frac{1}{2}$, which is its reciprocal, 2.

Divide Fractions

Name _____ Date _____

Example 1   One Common Factor

Find $\dfrac{5}{12} \div \dfrac{3}{8}$.

$\dfrac{5}{12} \div \dfrac{3}{8} = \dfrac{5}{12} \cdot \dfrac{8}{3}$ Rewrite the expression as a multiplication expression using the reciprocal of the divisor.

$= \dfrac{5}{12 \div 4} \cdot \dfrac{8 \div 4}{3}$ Divide the numerator 8 and the denominator 12 by the common factor 4.

$= \dfrac{5}{3} \cdot \dfrac{2}{3}$

$= \dfrac{5}{3} \cdot \dfrac{2}{3} = \dfrac{10}{9}$ Multiply.

$= 1\dfrac{1}{9}$ Express the improper fraction as a mixed number.

Example 2   More Than One Factor

Find $\dfrac{15}{24} \div \dfrac{30}{36}$.

$\dfrac{15}{24} \div \dfrac{30}{36} = \dfrac{15}{24} \cdot \dfrac{36}{30}$ Rewrite the expression as a multiplication expression using the reciprocal of the divisor.

$= \dfrac{15}{24 \div 12} \cdot \dfrac{36 \div 12}{30}$ Divide the numerator 36 and the denominator 24 by the common factor 12.

$= \dfrac{15}{2} \cdot \dfrac{3}{30}$

$= \dfrac{15 \div 15}{2} \cdot \dfrac{3}{30 \div 15}$ Divide the numerator 15 and the denominator 30 by the common factor 15.

$= \dfrac{1}{2} \cdot \dfrac{3}{2}$

$= \dfrac{3}{4}$ Multiply.

✓ Quick Check

Find each quotient. Write your answer in simplest form.

1 $\dfrac{3}{5} \div \dfrac{2}{10}$

2 $\dfrac{7}{12} \div \dfrac{3}{4}$

3 $\dfrac{7}{8} \div \dfrac{5}{12}$

Practice on Your Own
Find each quotient. Write your answer in simplest form.

4 $\dfrac{8}{9} \div \dfrac{2}{3}$

5 $\dfrac{2}{3} \div \dfrac{8}{9}$

6 $\dfrac{9}{10} \div \dfrac{3}{4}$

7 $\dfrac{8}{11} \div \dfrac{2}{5}$

8 $\dfrac{11}{18} \div \dfrac{5}{6}$

9 $\dfrac{3}{8} \div \dfrac{5}{12}$

Find the Quantity Represented by a Number of Units

TEACHING STRATEGY

1. **Vocabulary** Make sure students understand the meaning of *value*. **Ask** What does *value* mean? [a numerical amount or quantity]

2. **Teach** Direct students to Example 1. **Ask** Will the value you are asked to find, 3 units, be less than or greater than 250 miles? Why? [less than; 5 units is equal to 250 miles, and 3 units is less than 5 units, so the value of 3 units must be less than 250 miles.] Tell students that this strategy for solving problems is called the unitary method because it involves first finding the value of 1 unit. **Ask** How do we find the value of 1 unit? [Divide the total number of miles by the number of units: 250 miles ÷ 5 = 50 miles. So, 1 unit is 50 miles.] Now that we know the value of 1 unit, how do we find the value of 3 units? [Multiply the value of 1 unit by 3: 50 miles · 3 = 150 miles. So, 3 units is 150 miles.] Direct students to Example 1. **Ask** What information in the problem is used to create this bar model? [Five units represents 250 miles, so the whole bar is labeled 250 miles, and it is divided into 5 equal parts.] How can you use addition to confirm the value of 1 unit? [See if the sum of the values of 5 units is equal to the given value of 5 units: 50 + 50 + 50 + 50 + 50 = 250.] How can you use addition to confirm the value of 3 units? [See if the sum of the values of 3 units is equal to the value you found for 3 units: 50 + 50 + 50 = 150.]

Direct students to Example 2. **Ask** Will the value you are asked to find, 7 units, be less than or greater than 15 square inches? Why? [greater than; 3 units is equal to 15 square inches, and 7 units is greater than 3 units, so the value of 7 units must be greater than 15 square inches.] Point out to students that they are once again using the unitary method. **Ask** How do we find the value of 1 unit? [Divide the total number of square inches by the number of units: 15 square inches ÷ 3 = 5 square inches. So, 1 unit is 5 square inches.] Now that we know the value of 1 unit, how do we find the value of 7 units? [Multiply the value of 1 unit by 7 : 5 square inches · 7 = 35 square inches. So, 7 units is 35 square inches.]

Ask What information in the problem is used to create the bar model in Example 2? [Three units represents 15 square inches, so the whole bar is labeled 15 square inches, and it is divided into 3 equal parts.] How can you use addition to confirm the value of 1 unit? [See if the sum of the values of 3 units is equal to the given value of 3 units: 5 + 5 + 5 = 15]. How can you use addition to confirm the value of 7 units? [See if the sum of the values of 7 units is equal to the value you found for 7 units: 5 + 5 + 5 + 5 + 5 + 5 + 5 = 35.]

3. **Quick Check** Look for these common errors as students solve the Quick Check exercises.
   - Failure to find the value of 1 unit, indicating a lack of understanding of the unitary method.
   - Miscalculating the value of 1 unit, perhaps indicating confusion between dividends and divisors.
   - Forgetting to include units in their answers. indicating carelessness.

4. **Next Steps** Assign the practice exercises to students who show understanding.

Additional Teaching Resource

Online Transition Guide with Reteach and Extra Practice worksheets from previous grade levels

Find the Quantity Represented by a Number of Units

Example 1 Find Smaller Number of Units

If 5 units represent 250 miles, find the value of 3 units.

5 units → 250 miles

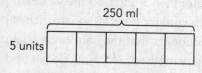

250 ml

5 units

$1 \text{ unit} \to \dfrac{250}{5} = 50 \text{ miles}$

50 ml

1 unit

3 units → 50 · 3 = 150 miles

150 ml

3 units

Example 2 Find Larger Number of Units

If 3 units represent 15 square inches, find the value of 7 units.

3 units → 15 square inches

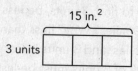

15 in.^{2}

3 units

$1 \text{ unit} \to \dfrac{15}{3} = 5 \text{ square inches}$

5 in.^{2}

1 unit

7 units → 5 · 7 = 35 square inches

35 in.^{2}

7 units

✓ Quick Check
Find the value of each set.

1 If 10 units represent 70 centimeters, find the value of 3 units.

2 If 4 units represent 24 quarts, find the value of 9 units

3 If 5 units represent 55 kilometers, find the value of 11 units.

_____   _____   _____

Practice on Your Own
Find the value of each set.

4 If 5 units represent 40 grams, find the value of 7 units.

5 If 7 units represent 56 feet, find the value of 8 units.

6 If 9 units represent 72 liters, find the value of 3 units.

_____   _____   _____

Find Ratios

TEACHING STRATEGY

1. **Vocabulary** Review the terms *ratio*, *equivalent*, *term*, and *simplest form*. **Ask** What is a ratio? [a comparison of two quantities] What does the term *equivalent* mean? [having the same value] Have students identify the terms of ratios on the student page. **Ask** When is a ratio in simplest form? [when the only common factor of the terms is 1]

2. **Teach** Direct students to Example 1. **Ask** How many ways can a ratio be written? [3] Direct students to Example 2. Remind students that to compare two quantities with different units, they must first convert one of the units. **Ask** How many centimeters are in 1 meter? [100] Direct students to Example 3. **Ask** Is there any limit to the number of equivalent ratios you can find by multiplying? [No, you can multiply both terms by any number and produce an equivalent ratio.] Direct students to Example 4. **Ask** Is there any limit to the number of equivalent ratios you can find by dividing? [Yes, you can only write an equivalent ratio for each factor besides 1 that the terms have in common.]

3. **Quick Check** Look for these common errors as students solve the Quick Check exercises.
   - Incorrectly converting units, indicating a lack of knowledge of conversion factors.
   - Failing to multiply or divide both terms of a ratio by the same number, indicating a lack of understanding of the role the Identity Properties play in writing equivalent ratios.

4. **Next Steps** Assign the practice exercises to students who show understanding. For students who need more support, provide tutoring using the alternate teaching strategy.

Additional Teaching Resource

Online Transition Guide with Reteach and Extra Practice worksheets from previous grade levels

ALTERNATE INTERVENTION STRATEGY

Materials: none

Strategy: Use a matching game to give students practice at recognizing and writing equivalent ratios and ratios in simplest form. You may have students play in groups of 2,3, or 4.

1. Prepare a set of ratio cards for each group of students. Each deck should contain 10 to 20 pairs of ratio cards. Each pair of cards should include two equivalent ratios. It is not necessary for one ratio in each pair to be in simplest form. The game can be made more interesting if some pairs are equivalent to other pairs.

2 : 3	6 : 9	18 : 24	3 : 4
6 : 8	30 : 40	5 : 2	15 : 6
7 : 11	2 : 66	14 : 22	28 : 44

2. Have students shuffle the cards and place them face down in a rectangular array. One student turns over two cards. He or she must tell whether the ratios are equivalent. If the student correctly identifies the ratios as nonequivalent, the cards are again turned face down, and he or she chooses which student goes next.

3. If the first student says the ratios are equivalent, he or she must use multiplication or division to prove on paper that they are. The student must also tell whether either of the ratios is in simplest form. If he or she is correct, the student keeps the cards and takes another turn. If he or she makes a mistake, the cards are again turned face down, and the student to his left takes a turn.

4. Play continues until there are no more cards left. The student with the most cards is the winner.

Find Ratios

You can use a ratio to compare two quantities that have the same units.

Example 1 **Same Units**

Find the ratio of length 27 inches to 4 inches.

This ratio can be expressed in three ways.

27 : 4   or   27 to 4   or $\frac{27}{4}$

Example 2 **Different Units**

Find the ratio of 17 centimeters to 5 meters.

17 cm : 5 m   cm and m are different units.

= 17 cm : 500 cm   Express 5 m as 500 cm.

This ratio can be expressed in three ways.

17 : 500   or   17 to 500   or $\frac{17}{500}$

When you multiply or divide both terms of a ratio, the result is an equivalent ratio.

Example 3 **Multiply to Find Equivalent Ratios**

4 : 5 ← simplest form

16 : 20

4 : 5 and 16 : 20 are equivalent ratios.

Example 4 **Divide to Find Equivalent Ratios**

9 : 12

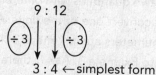

3 : 4 ← simplest form

9 : 12 and 3 : 4 are equivalent ratios.

✔ Quick Check

Express each ratio in simplest form.

1 3 in. : 5 ft _____

2 5 km : 40 m _____

Find two ratios equivalent to each ratio.

3 3 : 8 _____

4 9 : 10 _____

Practice on Your Own
Express each ratio in simplest form.

5 8 cm : 4 m _____

6 2 yd : 12 in. _____

Find two ratios equivalent to each ratio.

7 5 : 4 _____

8 11 : 12 _____

Find Equivalent Fractions Using Multiplication

TEACHING STRATEGY	ALTERNATE INTERVENTION STRATEGY

TEACHING STRATEGY

1. **Vocabulary** Remind students that *equivalent* means "equal in value."

2. **Teach** Work through the Example with students. In Step 2, rewrite $\frac{1 \cdot 5}{2 \cdot 5}$ as $\frac{1}{2} \cdot \frac{5}{5}$.

   Ask Multiplying by $\frac{5}{5}$ is the same as multiplying by what number? [1] Why does this result in an equivalent fraction? [Because when you multiply by 1, you do not change the value of the fraction.] Extend the Example by having students consider how to write an equivalent fraction for $\frac{1}{2}$ with a denominator of 100. **Ask** How can you express $\frac{1}{2}$ as an equivalent fraction with a denominator of 100 in just one step? [Multiply the numerator and denominator by 50: $\frac{1 \cdot 50}{2 \cdot 50} = \frac{50}{100}$.]

3. **Quick Check** Look for these common errors as students solve the Quick Check exercises.
   - Multiplying *either* the numerator or the denominator by another number.
   - Forgetting to multiply the numerator and denominator by the same number.

   These errors show a lack of understanding of the Identity Property of Multiplication. Multiplying a fraction by $\frac{a}{a}$ is the same as multiplying by 1, which results in a fraction with same value as the original fraction.

4. **Next Steps** Assign the practice exercises to students who show understanding. For students who need more support, provide tutoring using the alternate intervention strategy.

Additional Teaching Resource

 Online Transition Guide with Reteach and Extra Practice worksheets from previous grade levels

ALTERNATE INTERVENTION STRATEGY

Materials: none

Strategy: Use models to express equivalent fractions.

1. Write $\frac{1}{2} = \frac{5}{?}$ and draw the model shown below to represent $\frac{1}{2}$.

2. Tell students that in order to identify the missing denominator, they need to divide the model so that it shows 5 shaded parts. **Ask** What do we need to do to the model to show 5 shaded parts? [Draw 5 horizontal lines.] Divide the model as shown below.

3. Have students write the fraction represented by the model. **Ask** How many parts are there in all? [10] How many parts are shaded? [5] What fraction is represented by this model? $\left[\frac{5}{10}\right]$

4. Now write $\frac{5}{10} = \frac{?}{100}$. **Ask** What do we need to do to the model so that it shows 100 parts in all? [Divide the model so that it has 10 equal columns and 10 equal rows.] Divide the model as shown below.

Find Equivalent Fractions Using Multiplication

Example

Find the missing numerator and denominator.

$$\frac{1}{2} = \frac{5}{?} = \frac{?}{100}$$

STEP 1 To find the missing denominator, determine what number was multiplied by the numerator in the first fraction to result in the numerator of the second fraction.

Think: What number multiplied by 1 is equal to 5? $1 \cdot \mathbf{5} = 5$

STEP 2 Multiply the denominator in the first fraction by 5 to find the missing denominator.

$$\frac{1 \cdot 50}{2 \cdot 50} = \frac{5}{10}$$

STEP 3 To find the missing numerator, determine what number was multiplied by the denominator in the second fraction to result in the denominator of the third fraction.
Think: What number multiplied by 10 is equal to 100? $10 \cdot \mathbf{10} = 100$

STEP 4 Multiply the numerator in the second fraction by 10 to find the missing numerator.

$$\frac{5 \cdot 10}{10 \cdot 10} = \frac{50}{100}$$

✓ Quick Check

Find the missing numerators and denominators.

1 $\frac{1}{5} = \frac{10}{?} = \frac{?}{100}$

2 $\frac{1}{4} = \frac{5}{?} = \frac{?}{100}$

3 $\frac{7}{25} = \frac{14}{?} = \frac{?}{100}$

Practice on Your Own
Find the missing numerators and denominators.

4 $\frac{14}{25} = \frac{28}{?} = \frac{?}{100}$

5 $\frac{3}{4} = \frac{15}{?} = \frac{?}{100}$

6 $\frac{2}{5} = \frac{10}{?} = \frac{?}{100}$

7 $\frac{3}{10} = \frac{15}{?} = \frac{?}{100}$

8 $\frac{2}{2} = \frac{50}{?} = \frac{?}{100}$

9 $\frac{9}{10} = \frac{18}{?} = \frac{?}{100}$

Simplify Fractions Using Division

TEACHING STRATEGY

1. **Vocabulary** Review the meaning of *simplest form*. Write $\frac{3}{7}$. **Ask** Is $\frac{3}{7}$ in simplest form? Why or why not? [Yes, because 3 and 7 do not have any factors in common other than 1.] Is $\frac{6}{8}$ written in simplest form? Why or why not? [No, because 6 and 8 have a common factor of 2.]

2. **Teach** Explain to students that finding the greatest common factor of two numbers is the same thing as asking "What is the greatest number that will divide into the numerator and the denominator without a remainder?" **Ask** If you choose a factor that is not the greatest common factor, is the resulting fraction in simplest form? [No, you will have to simplify the fraction again to find the simplest form.] Review the example with students. Point out that if you divide the numerator and denominator by the common factor 2, the result is $\frac{16}{50}$, which is not in simplest form.

3. **Quick Check** Look for these common errors as students solve the Quick Check exercises.
   - Dividing by a common factor that is not the greatest common factor, yielding an answer that is a simplified fraction but is not in *simplest* form. This may indicate a lack of understanding of what simplest form is.
   - Dividing the numerator by one factor and the denominator by a different factor, indicating a lack of understanding of the role of the Identity Property of Division in simplifying fractions.

4. **Next Steps** Assign the practice exercises to students who show understanding. For students who need more support, provide tutoring using the alternate teaching strategy.

Additional Teaching Resource

Online Transition Guide with Reteach and Extra Practice worksheets from previous grade levels

ALTERNATE INTERVENTION STRATEGY

Materials: none

Strategy: Use repeated division by common factors to write a fraction in simplest form.

1. Explain to students that they can also use repeated division by common factors to express a fraction in simplest form.

2. Write $\frac{50}{100}$ on the board. **Ask** Besides 1, what is a common factor of both 50 and 100? [Possible answer: 2] What is 50 divided by 2? [25] What is 100 divided by 2? [50]

3. Write $\frac{50}{100} = \frac{50 \div 2}{100 \div 2} = \frac{25}{50}$ on the board. **Ask** Is $\frac{25}{50}$ in simplest form? [No.] Why not? [25 and 50 have other common factors besides 1.] **Ask** What number do you know that is easily divisible into 25 and 50? [5] What is 25 divided by 5? [5] What is 50 divided by 5? [10]

4. Write $\frac{25}{50} = \frac{25 \div 5}{50 \div 5} = \frac{5}{10}$ on the board. **Ask** Is $\frac{5}{10}$ in simplest form? [No.] **Ask** Besides 1, what is a common factor of both 5 and 10? [5] What is 5 divided by 5? [1] What is 10 divided by 5? [2]

5. Write $\frac{5}{10} = \frac{5 \div 5}{10 \div 5} = \frac{1}{2}$ on the board. **Ask** Is $\frac{1}{2}$ in simplest form? [Yes.] How do you know $\frac{1}{2}$ is in simplest form? [The only common factor of the numerator and denominator is 1.]

6. Repeat the activity to find the simplest forms of $\frac{40}{100}$ and $\frac{180}{240}$. $\left[\frac{2}{5} \text{ and } \frac{3}{4}\right]$

Simplify Fractions Using Division

Name _____ Date _____

Example

Express $\frac{32}{100}$ in simplest form.

STEP 1 List all the factors of the numerator and all the factors of the denominator.

numerator → 32 1, 2, 4, 8, 16, 32

denominator → $\overline{100}$ 1, 2, 4, 5, 10, 20, 25, 50, 100

STEP 2 Identify common factors.

numerator → 32 **1, 2, 4,** 8, 16, 32

denominator → $\overline{100}$ **1, 2, 4,** 5, 10, 20, 25, 50, 100

STEP 3 Identify the greatest common factor.

The greatest common factor of 32 and 100 is 4.

STEP 4 Divide both the numerator and the denominator by the greatest common factor.

$$\frac{32}{100} = \frac{32 \div 4}{100 \div 4} = \frac{8}{25}$$

$\frac{32}{100}$ expressed in simplest form is $\frac{8}{25}$.

✓ Quick Check

Express each fraction in simplest form.

1 $\frac{56}{100}$

2 $\frac{85}{100}$

3 $\frac{46}{100}$

_____ _____ _____

Practice on Your Own

Express each fraction in simplest form.

4 $\frac{50}{100}$

5 $\frac{25}{100}$

6 $\frac{72}{100}$

_____ _____ _____

7 $\frac{100}{150}$

8 $\frac{180}{300}$

9 $\frac{160}{280}$

_____ _____ _____

Write Fractions With a Denominator of 100 as Decimals

TEACHING STRATEGY

1. **Vocabulary** Make sure students understand the term *hundredth*. Say aloud "one hundredth." **Ask** Am I naming a fraction or a decimal? [You cannot tell.] Remind student that the fraction $\frac{1}{100}$ and the decimal 0.01 name the same value.

2. **Teach** Point out that fractions with a denominator of 100 can be easily written as decimals. Work through the examples with students. Explain that the fraction $\frac{14}{100}$ in Example 1 represents 14 hundredths, which is written as 0.14. **Ask** If the denominator is less than 100, how do you find an equivalent fraction? [Multiply both the numerator and denominator by the same number.] What if the denominator is greater than 100? [Divide the numerator and denominator by the same number.] Is it always possible to find an equivalent fraction with a denominator of 100? Explain. [Possible answer: No. It will only work when the denominator of the original fraction is a factor or multiple of 100.] In Example 2, point out that $\frac{30}{100}$ can be written as 0.30 or 0.3. For this chapter, students should be sure to include the zero in the hundredths place.

3. **Quick Check** Look for these common errors as students solve the Quick Check exercises.
   - Forgetting to multiply or divide the numerator and denominator by the same number.
   - Writing an equivalent decimal with the digits in the wrong decimal place (e.g., $\frac{2}{100} = 0.2$).

4. **Next Steps** Assign the practice exercises to students who show understanding. For students who need more support, provide tutoring using the alternate teaching strategy.

Additional Teaching Resource
Online Transition Guide with Reteach and Extra Practice worksheets from previous grade levels

ALTERNATE INTERVENTION STRATEGY

Materials: TRT13 (Decimal Squares)

Strategy: Use a hundreds grid to model equivalent fractions and decimals.

1. Guide students to understand that if they can write a fraction with a denominator of 100, then they can write an equivalent decimal.

2. Write $\frac{3}{4} = \frac{?}{100}$ on the board. **Ask** What number times 4 equals 100? [25] If we multiply the denominator by 25 to get 100, what must be do to the numerator? [Multiply it by 25.] What is the product of 3 and 25? [75]

3. Write $\frac{3}{4} = \frac{3 \cdot 25}{4 \cdot 25} = \frac{75}{100}$ on the board and display a hundreds grid. **Ask** There are 100 squares in this grid. Each square represents $\frac{1}{100}$. How many squares do you need to shade to model $\frac{75}{100}$? [Shade 75 squares.] Have a volunteer shade the hundreds grid.

4. **Ask** If each square represents 0.1, what decimal is modeled by the shaded grid? [0.75] Write $\frac{3}{4} = \frac{75}{100} = 0.75$ on the board.

5. Distribute hundreds grids. Repeat the activity using the fractions $\frac{4}{20}$ (0.20) and $\frac{27}{300}$ (0.09).

Write Fractions With a Denominator of 100 as Decimals

Example 1 — Denominator of 100

Express $\frac{14}{100}$ as a decimal.

When a fraction has a denominator of 100, write the number of hundredths shown in the numerator in decimal form.

$\frac{14}{100} = 14$ hundredths $= 0.14$

Example 2 — Denominator less than 100

Express $\frac{6}{20}$ as a decimal.

STEP 1 Write an equivalent fraction that has a denominator of 100.

$\frac{6}{20} = \frac{6 \times 5}{20 \times 5} = \frac{30}{100}$

STEP 2 Write the equivalent fraction as a decimal.

$\frac{30}{100} = 30$ hundredths $= 0.30$

Example 3 — Denominator greater than 100

Express $\frac{88}{400}$ as a decimal.

STEP 1 Write an equivalent fraction that has a denominator of 100.

$\frac{88}{400} = \frac{88 \div 4}{400 \div 4} = \frac{22}{100}$

STEP 2 Write the equivalent fraction as a decimal.

$\frac{22}{100} = 22$ hundredths $= 0.22$

✔ Quick Check

Express each fraction as a decimal.

1 $\frac{8}{10}$

2 $\frac{65}{100}$

3 $\frac{72}{200}$

_____

Practice on Your Own
Express each fraction as a decimal.

4 $\frac{42}{600}$

5 $\frac{27}{50}$

6 $\frac{1}{2}$

_____

7 $\frac{23}{100}$

8 $\frac{30}{500}$

9 $\frac{11}{25}$

_____

Multiply Fractions by Whole Numbers

TEACHING STRATEGY

1. **Vocabulary** Make sure students understand the term *common factor*. **Ask** What are the common factors of 12 and 16? [1, 2, and 4] Then, using the worksheet, have volunteers identify examples of the following terms: *numerator, denominator, improper fraction,* and *mixed number.*

2. **Teach** Work through the Examples with students. In each Example, make sure that students understand that you divide both the denominator and the whole number in the expression by a common factor. **Ask** How does dividing by a common factor help you multiply a fraction by a whole number? [Possible answer: It makes the numbers easier to work with and compute.] Remind students that they should write any improper fractions as mixed numbers in their answers. **Ask** How do you write the improper fraction $\frac{28}{3}$ as a mixed number? [Divide the numerator by the denominator: $28 \div 3 = 9$ R1 or $9\frac{1}{3}$.]

3. **Quick Check** Look for these common errors as students solve the Quick Check exercises.
   - Neglecting to write an improper fraction as a mixed number.
   - Forgetting to divide by a common factor, when possible.

4. **Next Steps** Assign the practice exercises to students who show understanding. For students who need more support, provide tutoring using the alternate teaching strategy.

Additional Teaching Resource

Online Transition Guide with Reteach and Extra Practice worksheets from previous grade levels

Materials: none

Strategy: Use models to multiply fractions by a whole number.

1. Write $\frac{2}{3} \cdot 12$ on the board. Then draw a bar model to illustrate $\frac{2}{3}$ of the whole, 12. Explain to students that $\frac{2}{3}$ means 2 units of out 3 units.

2. To find the product of $\frac{2}{3} \cdot 12$, students find the value of 1 part, or unit, first. **Ask** What is the value of all 3 parts? [12] How could you find the value of 1 part? [Divide 12 by 3.] What is the value of 1 part? [4]

3. Students now find the value of 2 parts. **Ask** If 1 part has a value of 4, what is the value of 2 parts? [2 · 4, or 8 parts] What is the product of $\frac{2}{3} \cdot 12$? [8]

5. Repeat the activity for $\frac{3}{8} \cdot 32$. Students should understand that 8 parts have a value of 32 and that 1 part has a value of 32 ÷ 8, or 4. Therefore, 3 parts have a value of 3 · 4, or 12.

6. Once students are comfortable with using models to multiply fractions by a whole number, help them connect this process to the ones shown in the examples on the student page.

Multiply Fractions by Whole Numbers

Example 1

Find $\frac{3}{5} \cdot 35$.

STEP 1 Identify the common factors of the denominator, 5, and the factor 35.

5: 1, **5**   35: 1, **5**, 7, 35

STEP 2 Divide by the common factor 5.

$$\frac{3}{5} \cdot 35 = \frac{3}{5 \div 5} \cdot (35 \div 5) = \frac{3}{1} \cdot 7$$

STEP 3 Multiply.

$$\frac{3}{1} \cdot 7 = \frac{3 \cdot 7}{1} = \frac{21}{1} = 21$$

Example 2

Find $\frac{4}{9} \cdot 21$.

STEP 1 Identify the common factors of the denominator, 9, and the factor 21.

9: 1, **3**, 9   21: 1, **3**, 7, 21

STEP 2 Divide by the common factor 3.

$$\frac{4}{9} \cdot 21 = \frac{4}{9 \div 3} \cdot (21 \div 3) = \frac{4}{3} \cdot 7$$

STEP 3 Multiply.

$$\frac{4}{3} \cdot 7 = \frac{4 \cdot 7}{3} = \frac{28}{3}$$

STEP 4 Write as a mixed number.

$$\frac{28}{3} = 9\frac{1}{3}$$

✔ Quick Check
Find each product.

1 $\frac{4}{5} \cdot 40$

2 $\frac{5}{6} \cdot 9$

3 $\frac{1}{2} \cdot 18$

_____   _____   _____

Practice on Your Own
Find each product.

4 $\frac{3}{4} \cdot 30$

5 $\frac{2}{5} \cdot 20$

6 $\frac{2}{7} \cdot 63$

_____   _____   _____

7 $\frac{5}{9} \cdot 51$

8 $\frac{7}{10} \cdot 45$

9 $\frac{3}{8} \cdot 26$

_____   _____   _____

Use Bar Models to Show the Four Operations

TEACHING STRATEGY

1. **Vocabulary** Make sure students understand what it means to model an operation. **Ask** Where have you seen or heard the term *model* before? What does *model* mean in those contexts? [Possible answers: model cars, houses, planes, or trains; clay figures; A model is a representation of an object or idea.]

2. **Teach** Introduce bar models for addition and subtraction as *part-part-whole models*. Explain that when we use bar models for addition and subtraction we are trying to identify different parts of the bar. The size of one of the smaller parts may be unknown, or the size of the whole bar may be unknown. Refer to the bar model in Example 1.

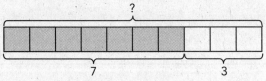

Say When we add 7 + 3, we know the size of the smaller parts of the bar. **Ask** What don't we know? What are we trying to find? [Answer: the length of the whole bar] Refer to the bar model in Example 2.

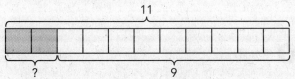

Say When we subtract 11 − 9, we know the size of the whole bar and one of the smaller parts. **Ask** What is unknown? What are we trying to find? [Answer: the length of one of the parts of the bar]

Explain that bar models for multiplication and division show bars that are divided into equal parts. The size of the whole bar may be unknown. The number of parts may be unknown.

Or the size of each part (or group) may be unknown.

Refer to the bar model in Example 3.

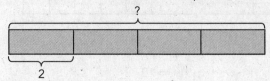

Say When we multiply 4 × 2, we know the number of equal parts (4) and the size of each part (2). **Ask** What don't we know? What are we trying to find? [Answer: the length of the whole bar] Explain to students that when using a bar to model multiplication, they can choose which factor to represent as the number of equal parts and which one to use to represent the size of each part. Model 4 × 2 again, using a bar divided into 2 equal parts with lengths of 4. Show that the answer is the same. Refer to the bar model in Example 4.

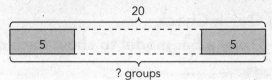

Say When we divide 20 ÷ 5, we know the size of the whole bar (20) and the size of each part (5). **Ask** What don't we know? What are we trying to find? [Answer: the number of equal parts in the bar]

3. **Quick Check** Look for these common errors as students solve the Quick Check exercises.
   - Adding the two numbers in a subtraction problem, indicating a poor understanding of the part-part-whole model.
   - In a division problem, confusing the number of parts with the size of each part, indicating a lack of understanding for the two possibilities for division.

4. **Next Steps** Assign the practice exercises to students who show understanding.

Additional Teaching Resource

🖱 Online Transition Guide with Reteach and Extra Practice worksheets from previous grade levels

Name _____   Date _____

Use Bar Models to Show the Four Operations

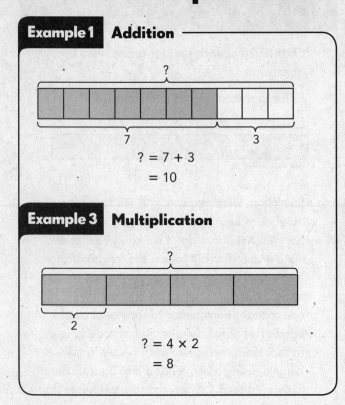

Example 1 **Addition**

?

7   3

? = 7 + 3
  = 10

Example 3 **Multiplication**

?

2

? = 4 × 2
  = 8

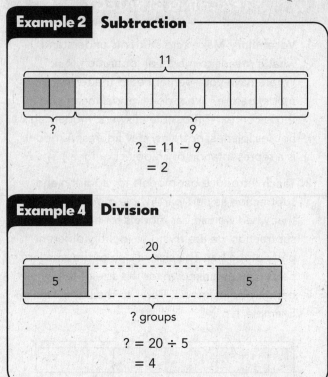

Example 2 **Subtraction**

11

?   9

? = 11 − 9
  = 2

Example 4 **Division**

20

5   5

? groups

? = 20 ÷ 5
  = 4

✓ Quick Check

Draw a bar model to show each operation.

1 15 − 4

2 13 + 4

3 30 ÷ 6

4 7 × 4

Practice on Your Own

Draw a bar model to show each operation. Write the result of each operation.

5 33 ÷ 3

5 11 + 7

7 5 × 7

8 19 − 9

Find Common Factors and Greatest Common Factors

TEACHING STRATEGY

1. **Vocabulary** Make sure students understand the terms *factor*, *common factor*, and *greatest common factor*, as well as how the three terms are related. Have students choose a pair of numbers, and list all of their factors. Then have students identify the common factors, and finally, have them identify the greatest common factor. Have students explain their answers.

2. **Teach** Use definitions students have made and refined to identify factors of 8 and 12. Then have students list the factors of each in order, identify factors common to both lists, and finally identify the greatest common factor.
Ask What is the least number of factors a number can have? What are these factors? [Answers: two; 1 and the number itself] **Ask** What is the name for a number that only has two factors? [Answer: a prime number] **Ask** Do either 8 or 12 have only two factors? Explain. [Answer: No, both 8 and 12 have more than 2 factors. So, 8 and 12 are not prime numbers.]

3. **Quick Check** Look for these common errors as students solve the Quick Check exercises.
   - Choosing the greatest factor in either list rather than the greatest common factor, indicating confusion about common factors.
   - When listing factors of a number, omitting 1 and/or the number itself, indicating an incomplete understanding of what factors are.

4. **Next Steps** Assign the practice exercises to students who show understanding. For students who need more support, provide tutoring using the alternate teaching strategy.

Additional Teaching Resource

Online Transition Guide with Reteach and Extra Practice worksheets from previous grade levels

ALTERNATE INTERVENTION STRATEGY

Materials: colored pencils

Strategy: Use prime factorization to find the greatest common factor of two numbers.

1. Remind students that a prime number is a number that has only two factors, itself and 1. (1 is not a prime number.) A prime factor of a number is a factor that is a prime number.

2. Find the greatest common factor of 8 and 12 by using prime factorization. Follow these steps:
   - Choose any two factors of 8 and of 12. Continue to factor the factors until all the factors are prime.

$$
\begin{array}{cc}
8 & 12 \\
/\backslash & /\backslash \\
2 \times 4 & 2 \times 6 \\
/\backslash & /\backslash \\
2 \times 2 & 2 \times 3
\end{array}
$$

   - Write 8 and 12 as products of prime factors, listing factors in order from least to greatest. Then circle matching pairs of prime numbers.

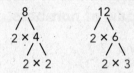

$$
8 = 2 \times 2 \times 2
$$
$$
12 = 2 \times 2 \times 3
$$

   - Explain that the greatest common factor of 8 and 12 is the product of the matched pairs.

$$
2 \times 2 = 4
$$

So, the greatest common factor of 8 and 12 is 4.

3. Work through other examples with students using prime factorization (e.g., try 6 and 12, whose matched pairs are 2 and 3; 3 and 15, whose only matched pair is 3; 16 and 48, whose matched pairs are 2, 2, 2 and 2).

Name _____ Date _____

Find Common Factors and Greatest Common Factors

Example

List the common factors of 8 and 12, and then find their greatest common factor.

STEP 1 Identify all the factors of 8 and all the factors of 12.

$$8 = 1 \times 8 \qquad\qquad 12 = 1 \times 12$$
$$ = 2 \times 4 \qquad\qquad = 2 \times 6$$
$$ = 3 \times 4$$

Factors of 8: 1, 2, 4, and 8   Factors of 12: 1, 2, 3, 4, 6, and 12

STEP 2 The common factors of 8 and 12: 1, 2, and 4

STEP 3 The greatest common factor of 8 and 12 is 4.

☑ Quick Check

Find the common factors and greatest common factor of each pair of numbers.

1 6 and 12

_____

2 4 and 10

_____

3 3 and 15

_____

4 24 and 36

_____

Practice on Your Own

Find the common factors and greatest common factor of each pair of numbers.

5 12 and 24

_____

6 10 and 25

_____

7 8 and 20

_____

8 9 and 33

_____

9 18 and 30

_____

10 9 and 16

_____

Understand Mathematical Terms

TEACHING STRATEGY

1. **Vocabulary** Make sure students understand the terms *sum*, *difference*, *product*, *dividend*, *divisor*, and *quotient*. In particular, emphasize how *dividend* and *divisor* are different. Have students work in pairs. One partner writes addition, subtraction, multiplication, and division exercises, and the other partner labels the parts of each. Students then switch roles.

2. **Teach** Introduce each term with an example. Then have students write their own examples and identify the parts. **Ask** What symbol helps you identify a sum? A difference? A product? A quotient? [Answers: +; −; ×; ÷] **Ask** Which comes first in a division expression that uses a division sign , the dividend or the divisor? [Answer: the dividend] **Ask** Which comes immediately after the division sign? [Answer: the divisor]

3. **Quick Check** Look for these common errors as students solve the quick check exercises.
   - In a division example, confusing *dividend* and *divisor*, indicating a misunderstanding of the meanings of those terms.
   - Confusing *sum*, *difference*, *product*, or *quotient*, indicating confusion about the names of the results of different operations.

4. **Next Steps** Assign the practice exercises to students who show understanding. For students who need more support, provide tutoring using the alternate teaching strategy.

Additional Teaching Resource

Online Transition Guide with Reteach and Extra Practice worksheets from previous grade levels

ALTERNATE INTERVENTION STRATEGY

Materials: Use TRT12 (Grid Paper) to make a crossword puzzle as shown below.

Strategy: Use exercises to identify terms, and record terms in a simple crossword puzzle.

1. Have students use the clues to identify terms.

   ACROSS
   1) number being divided: $\boxed{25} \div 5$
   _____
   4) result of adding: 5 + 8 _____
   5) result of multiplying: 9 × 5 _____
   DOWN
   1) number doing the dividing: $25 \div \boxed{5}$
   _____
   2) result of subtracting: 19 − 4 _____
   3) result of dividing: 25 ÷ 5 _____

2. After each term is identified, have students place it in the proper place in the crossword puzzle.

3. Have interested students write their own examples for the terms and create their own crossword puzzles.

Understand Mathematical Terms

Example 1 Addition

When you add, the result is called the *sum*. For example, the sum of 5 and 4 is 5 + 4.

sum: 5 + 4

Example 2 Subtraction

When you subtract, the result is called the *difference*. For example, the difference of 9 and 2 is 9 − 2.

difference: 9 − 2

Example 3 Multiplication

When you multiply, the result is called the *product*. For example, the product of 5 and 7 is 5 × 7.

product: 5 × 7

Example 4 Division

When you divide, the result is called the *quotient*. For example, the quotient of 12 and 4 is $\frac{12}{4}$.

quotient: $\frac{12}{4}$
or
12 ÷ 4

The number you are dividing is called the *dividend*. The number you are dividing by is called the *divisor*.

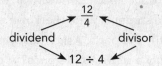

dividend   divisor

12 ÷ 4

✔ Quick Check

Complete with *quotient*, *sum*, *difference*, *product*, *dividend*, or *divisor*.

1 The _____ of 8 and 4 is 8 × 4.

2 The _____ of 9 and 3 is $\frac{9}{3}$. 9 is the _____ and 3 is the _____.

3 The _____ of 7 and 3 is 7 − 3.

4 The _____ of 6 and 2 is 6 + 2.

Practice on Your Own
Complete with *quotient*, *sum*, *difference*, *product*, *dividend*, or *divisor*.

5 The _____ of 19 and 7 is 19 − 7.

6 The _____ of 18 and 7 is 18 + 7.

7 The _____ of 8 and 7 is 8 × 7.

8 The _____ of 15 and 5 is 15 ÷ 5. 5 is the _____ and 15 is the _____.

Compare Numbers Using > and <

TEACHING STRATEGY

1. **Vocabulary** Draw the symbols =, >, and < on the board. Have students explain the meaning of each symbol. Make sure students can differentiate between > and <, reinforcing the idea that the symbol always opens to the greater number.

2. **Teach** Explain to students that it is not always necessary to solve expressions in order to compare the numbers in the exercises. **Ask** If you are comparing a negative number and a positive number, what is always true? [Answer: The positive number is always greater.] **Ask** If you are comparing two negative numbers, what is always true? [Answer: The number with the greater absolute value is less than the other number.] **Ask** Without multiplying, how do you know that $6 + 6 + 6$ is equal to $3 \cdot 6$? [Answer: Since multiplication is repeated division, you know that writing $3 \cdot 6$ is the same as writing $6 + 6 + 6$.]

3. **Quick Check** Look for these common errors as students solve the Quick Check exercises.
   - Confusing the symbols > (is greater than) and < (is less than).
   - Mistaking the values of negative numbers (i.e., assuming that $-34 > -30$ because $34 > 30$).

4. **Next Steps** Assign the practice exercises to students who show understanding. For students who need more support, provide tutoring using the alternate teaching strategy.

Additional Teaching Resource

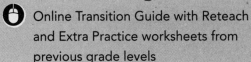 Online Transition Guide with Reteach and Extra Practice worksheets from previous grade levels

ALTERNATE INTERVENTION STRATEGY

Materials: TRT7 (Negative Number Lines)

Strategy: Use a number line to help compare numbers.

1. Remind students that on a horizontal number line numbers increase in value from left to right. For vertical number lines, numbers increase in value from the bottom to the top. Negative numbers appear to the left of 0 and positive numbers to the right of 0.

2. Compare -8 and -10 using a horizontal number line. Follow these steps:
   - Draw a number line divided into 10 equal sections. Label the number line from -10 to 0.

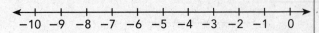

   - Plot the points for -8 and -10 on the number line.

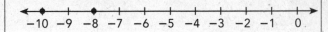

   - Point out that -8 is to the right of -10 on the number line, so it has a greater value.

   Therefore, $-8 > -10$.

3. Work through other examples with students, including examples where they first need to evaluate expressions. Have students use number lines on their own to compare the numbers and expressions.

Name _____   Date _____

Compare Numbers Using > and <

Example 1   Comparing Numbers

Complete with =, >, or <.

−42 [?] 24

−42 [?] 24   Compare the numbers. First, check
the sign of each number.

−42 < 24   The first number is negative and the
second is positive. Therefore, the
negative number is less than the
positive number.

Example 2   Comparing Expressions

Complete with +, >, or <.

16 × 4 [?] 16 ÷ 4

64 [?] 4   Evaluate each expression.

64 > 4   Compare the numbers.

✓ Quick Check

Complete with =, >, or <.

1 36 [?] −38

2 −34 [?] −30

3 36 ÷ 6 [?] 6 ÷ 36

4 27 [?] 3 · 3 · 3

Practice on Your Own
Complete with =, >, or <.

5 12 · 6 [?] 74

6 −39 [?] −89

7 4 · 4 [?] 8 · 2

8 3 [?] −289

9 −19 [?] −16

8 25 [?] 25^2

11 18 [?] −18

12 $\sqrt{81}$ [?] 9

13 4 · 3 [?] 3 + 4

Use Variables to Write Algebraic Expressions

TEACHING STRATEGY

1. **Vocabulary** Make sure students understand the terms *variable* and *expression*. If students confuse the terms *expression* and *equation*, ask a volunteer to explain the difference. Students should understand that an expression does not contain an equal sign, while an equation does.

2. **Teach** Point out to students that an algebraic expression is a mathematical way of writing a word phrase. Explain that associating key words with the correct operation is critical to being able to make the connection between words and algebra. Provide students with examples of simple phrases and real-life situations. **Ask** What operation is described in the phrase the product of x and 18? Explain. [Answer: Multiplication; the key word *product* indicates multiplication is used and x and 18 are the factors in the expression.] **Ask** If you are x years old and your sister is 5 years older, what expression could you write to show your sister's age? [Answer: $x + 5$]

3. **Quick Check** Look for this common error as students solve the Quick Check exercises.
   • Using the wrong operation in an expression as a result of misunderstanding key words and the operations associated with them.

4. **Next Steps** Assign the practice exercises to students who show understanding. For students who need more support, provide tutoring using the alternate teaching strategy.

Additional Teaching Resource
Online Transition Guide with Reteach and Extra Practice worksheets from previous grade levels

ALTERNATE INTERVENTION STRATEGY

Materials: index cards

Strategy: Use index cards to write algebraic expressions for a word expression.

1. Write on each index card a numeric expression such as: $6 + 4, 7 - 3, 4 \cdot 2$, and $18 \div 9$.

2. Divide students into groups of four.
   • Have one student hold up an index card.
   • Have each student in the group read aloud the expression.
   • Try to get students to use as many different phrases as possible. For example, "6 + 4" can be read as *6 plus 4*, *the sum of 6 and 4*, *4 added to 6*, and so on.
   • Ask students to record each phrase on an index card.

3. For each expression, have students replace one of the numbers with a variable. For example:
   $a + 4, 7 - b, 4 \cdot t$, and $m \div 9$.

4. Again, have students in each group read the expression aloud using different phrases. Record each phrase on an index card.

5. Remove the algebraic expressions. Distribute the index cards with the algebraic expressions in word form and have students write the algebraic form.

Use Variables to Write Algebraic Expressions

Name _____ Date _____

Example 1

Write an algebraic expression for the following.

   The product of p and 30

The word *product* indicates multiplication. So p and 30 are factors in the expression: $p \cdot 30$.

A product of a number and a variable can be rewritten as a single term. The number is written before the variable.

   $30p$

Example 2

Write an algebraic expression for the following.

   The sum of 28 and x

The word *sum* indicates addition. So 28 and x are addends in the expression.

   $28 + x$

✔ Quick Check

Write an algebraic expression for each of the following.

1 Divide 16 by y.

_____

2 The product of s and 13

_____

3 Subtract 5 from t.

_____

4 The sum of 34 and c

_____

Practice on Your Own
Write an algebraic expression for each of the following.

5 Subtract y from 7.

_____

6 The sum of 10 and x

_____

7 The product of d and 56

_____

8 Divide m by 9.

_____

Evaluate Algebraic Expressions

TEACHING STRATEGY

1. **Vocabulary** Explain that an algebraic expression is similar to a numerical expression, but an algebraic expression contains numbers and one or more variables. Make sure students understand the terms *substitute* and *evaluate*. Explain that to substitute a value into an expression is to replace a variable with a given value (a number). Evaluating an expression means to substitute a given value for the variable and then simplify the expression.

2. **Teach** Review the order of operations with students and point out that they will need to follow the rules to correctly simplify expressions. Have students consider the first part of the Example. **Ask** What two operations will be used to simplify this expression? [Multiplication then subtraction.] **Ask** What number replaces x? [8] Work through the first part of the Example. Point out what happens when you do not follow the correct order of operations. If you subtract before multiplying, $5 \cdot 8 - 5$ results in $5 \cdot 3 = 15$, which is an incorrect answer.

3. **Quick Check** Look for this common error as students solve the Quick Check exercises.
   - Adding or subtracting before multiplying or dividing, indicating unfamiliarity with the correct order of operations.
   - Multiplying when x appears, indicating confusion between the variable x and the multiplication symbol $\times$.

4. **Next Steps** Assign the practice exercises to students who show understanding. For students who need more support, provide tutoring using the alternate teaching strategy.

> **Additional Teaching Resource**
> 🖱 Online Transition Guide with Reteach and Extra Practice worksheets from previous grade levels

ALTERNATE INTERVENTION STRATEGY

Materials: none

Strategy: Use a table format to evaluate a single expression for several values.

1. Create the table below on the board and have students duplicate it. Tell students they are going to evaluate an expression for several different values.

Value	Substitution	Simplification
0	6(___) + 3	___ + 3 = ___
1	6(___) + 3	___ + 3 = ___
2	6(___) + 3	___ + 3 = ___
3	6(___) + 3	___ + 3 = ___
4	6(___) + 3	___ + 3 = ___

2. Have students complete the table by filling in the blanks and then have them check their answers. **Ask** Based on the center column, what algebraic expression are you evaluating? Use the variable x in your expression. [$6x + 3$]

3. Have students duplicate the table below, identify the expression, and complete the last two columns. [Expression is $4x - 5$.]

Value	Substitution	Simplification
2	4( ) − 5	___ − 5 = ___
4	4( ) − 5	___ − 5 = ___
6	4( ) − 5	___ − 5 = ___
8	4( ) − 5	___ − 5 = ___
10	4( ) − 5	___ − 5 = ___

4. When students are comfortable completing tables, give them other algebraic expressions and have them create their own tables using the given values 0, 1, 2, 3, and 4.

Evaluate Algebraic Expressions

Example

Evaluate $5x - 5$ when $x = 8$ and $x = 10$.

When $x = 8$:

STEP 1 Substitute. Replace the variable x in the expression with the value 8.

$5x - 5 = 5 \cdot 8 - 5$

STEP 2 According to the order of operations, multiply before subtracting.

$5 \cdot 8 - 5 = 40 - 5$

STEP 3 Subtract.

$40 - 5 = 35$

When $x = 10$:

STEP 1 Substitute. Replace the variable x in the expression with the value 10.

$5x - 5 = 5 \cdot 10 - 5$

STEP 2 According to the order of operations, multiply before subtracting.

$5 \cdot 10 - 5 = 50 - 5$

STEP 3 Subtract.

$50 - 5 = 45$

☑ **Quick Check**

Evaluate each expression for the given values of the variable.

1 $2y + 7$ when $y = 5$ and $y = 8$

2 $\frac{36}{x}$ when $x = 4$ and $x = 6$

3 $32 - 3x$ when $x = 6$ and $x = 10$

4 $\frac{y}{2} - 3$ when $y = 6$ and $y = 14$

Practice on Your Own
Evaluate each expression for the given values of the variable.

5 $32 - 2y$ when $y = 5$ and $y = 12$

6 $6x + 12$ when $x = 1$ and $x = 9$

7 $40 - 4x$ when $x = 2$ and $x = 7$

8 $2y + 7$ when $y = 0$ and $y = 14$

Plot Points on a Coordinate Plane

TEACHING STRATEGY

1. **Vocabulary** Make sure students understand the terms *x-axis* and *y-axis* and can distinguish between the two. Display Quadrant I (See TRT16.) of the coordinate plane and have students identify the x-axis and the y-axis. If students have difficulty, tell them to remember, "The y-axis points up high."

2. **Teach** Explain to students that the numbers in an ordered pair are called *coordinates* and they give the location of a point on the coordinate plane. The first number is called the x-coordinate and the second number is called the y-coordinate. **Ask** Which number in an ordered pair tells you how far to move to the right from the origin? [the first number] Which number tells you how far to move up from the origin? [the second number] Stress the importance of always starting at the origin when plotting points on a coordinate plane. The origin represents the point at which the x-axis and y-axis intersect and is named by the ordered pair (0, 0). Display a coordinate plane and label the point (3, 6) as point *D*. **Ask** What ordered pair names point *A*? [(3, 6)] Then work through the example with students.

3. **Quick Check** Look for these common errors as students solve the Quick Check exercises.
   - Confusing the x-coordinates and y-coordinates in ordered pairs.
   - Beginning at a point other than zero when counting units for each coordinate in an ordered pair.

4. **Next Steps** Assign the practice exercises to students who show understanding. For students who need more support, provide tutoring using the alternate teaching strategy.

Additional Teaching Resource

 Online Transition Guide with Reteach and Extra Practice worksheets from previous grade levels

ALTERNATE INTERVENTION STRATEGY

Materials: index cards with ordered pairs, TRT17 (Coordinate Grids)

Strategy: Use a kinesthetic model to plot points.

1. Prepare a set of cards with ordered pairs. The ordered pairs should not be larger than (5, 5).

2. Arrange classroom chairs or other objects (such as books) into 6 rows and 6 columns as shown below.

3. Explain to students that the array is a coordinate plane. **Ask** Where is the starting point on a coordinate plane? [The origin or (0, 0)] Have a student sit in the chair or stand at the object located at the origin.

4. Have the student take one of the cards and read the ordered pair on the card. The student should move to the chair located at the point on the card. Stress the need to move right and then up to the point.

5. Repeat the activity several times. When students show an understanding of moving to the correct locations, reverse the activity. Place a student somewhere on the "plane" and have another student name the ordered pair that describes the point.

6. When students show an understanding, have them try the exercise by plotting the points on graph paper.

Name _____ Date _____

Plot Points on a Coordinate Plane

Example

Plot the points A (1, 5), B (7, 2), and C (6, 6).

STEP 1 To plot point A (1, 5), move 1 unit to the right of 0 on the x-axis and 5 units above 0 on the y-axis.

STEP 1 To plot point B (7, 2), move 7 units to the right of 0 on the x-axis and 2 units above 0 on the y-axis.

STEP 1 To plot point C (6, 6), move 6 units to the right of 0 on the x-axis and 6 units above 0 on the y-axis.

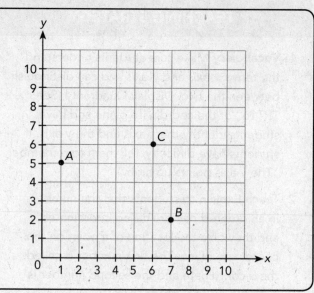

✓ Quick Check

Plot the points on the coordinate plane at right.

1 A (4, 3)

2 B (2, 4)

3 C (3, 2)

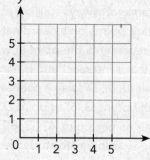

Practice on Your Own
Plot the points on the coordinate plane at right.

4 A (8, 2)

5 B (3, 10)

6 C (5, 5)

7 D (4, 9)

8 E (9, 4)

9 F (7, 1)

10 G (6, 7)

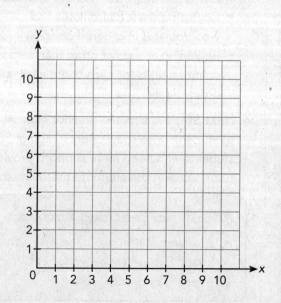

Identify and Plot Coordinates

TEACHING STRATEGY

1. **Vocabulary** Using the worksheet, have students identify examples of the following terms: *coordinates*, x-*axis*, y-*axis*, and *origin*.

2. **Teach** Work through the steps of the example with students. **Ask** Why is the point O at (0, 0) called the origin? [It is where you start to locate all points on the coordinate plane.] **Ask** Which coordinate in an ordered pair shows the distance along the x-axis from the origin? [the first] **Ask** Which coordinate in an ordered pair shows the distance along the y-axis from the origin? [the second] Then, direct students to Step 3. To locate B, move right 4 units along the x-axis and up 1 unit on the y-axis. **Ask** What information displayed on the coordinate plane shows direction? [The arrows on the axes show direction.] In which direction does the x-axis point? [It points to the right.] In which direction does the y-axis point? [It points up.]

3. **Quick Check** Look for these common errors as students solve the Quick Check exercises.
   - Transposing the x- and y-coordinates indicating a misunderstanding of coordinate notation.
   - Not understanding the location of the 0 coordinates at the origin as they relate to the x- or y-axis, indicating confusion about the role of the axes.

4. **Next Steps** Assign the practice exercises to students who show understanding. For students who need more support, provide tutoring using the alternate teaching strategy.

Additional Teaching Resource

Online Transition Guide with Reteach and Extra Practice worksheets from previous grade levels

ALTERNATE INTERVENTION STRATEGY

Materials: index cards, red and blue markers, TRT16 (Coordinate Grid) for display and TRT17 (Coordinate Grids) for students

Strategy: Create ordered pairs to identify and plot points in the coordinate plane.

1. Create 2 decks of index cards with 10 cards each. Number the cards in one deck from 1 to 10 in red. Number the cards in the other deck from 1 to 10 in blue.

2. Display a coordinate plane that is easily accessible to students.

3. Explain to students that the "red" cards are the x-coordinates and the "blue" cards are the y-coordinates.

4. Have students draw a card from each deck to create an ordered pair. Ask them to explain which coordinate comes first and which comes second. [red x-coordinate, blue y-coordinate]

5. After students have correctly identified the ordered pair, have them plot the coordinates as a point on the coordinate plane. They can label the point with the initial of their first name.

6. Ask students to explain the process for plotting a point. Guide them with questions, such as "What does the first coordinate tell you to do?" [Move right from the origin along the x-axis.] "What does the second coordinate tell you to do? [Move up from the origin along the y-axis.]

7. Continue to have students draw ordered pairs until all cards in both decks have been used.

Identify and Plot Coordinates

Example

Use the coordinate plane at right to identify and plot points.

STEP 1 Identify the coordinates of O, the origin. O is 0 units on both the x-axis and the y-axis; its coordinates are (0, 0).

STEP 2 Identify the location of point A. A is 3 units right on the x-axis and 2 units up on the y-axis; its coordinates are (3, 2).

STEP 3 Plot point B at (4, 1) on the grid. 4 units right on the x-axis; 1 unit up on the y-axis.

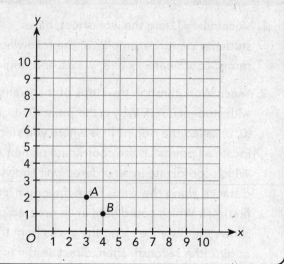

✓ Quick Check

Use the coordinate plane at right.
Name the coordinates of each point.

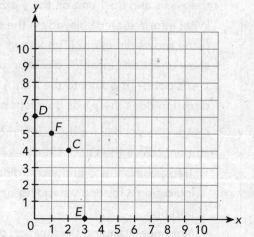

1 C _____

2 D _____

3 E _____

4 F _____

Practice on Your Own
Use the coordinate plane at right.
Name the coordinates of each point.

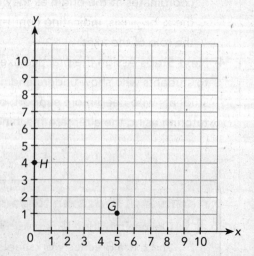

5 G _____

6 H _____

Plot the following points on the coordinate plane.

7 J (1, 1)

8 K (3, 5)

Represent Negative Numbers on a Number Line

TEACHING STRATEGY

1. **Vocabulary** Make sure students understand the term *negative* and that negative numbers are to the left of 0 on a horizontal number line. Remind them that negative numbers are values less than 0 and preceded by a negative sign.

2. **Teach** Review how to locate positive numbers on the number line. As students work through Step 2 of the Example, have them draw 5 counting arrows to the left of 0 to help them visualize the distance from 0 as they locate 5. **Ask** Looking at the number line, how are 5 and −5 alike? [They are both the same distance from 0.] How are they different? [They are found in opposite directions. 5 is to the right of 0, and −5 is to the left of 0.] **Ask** Where have you seen negative numbers used? [Possible answers: very cold temperatures, distances below sea level, withdrawals from a bank account] **Ask** What information displayed on the number line shows direction? [The arrows at each end of the number line show direction.]

3. **Quick Check** Look for these common errors as students solve the Quick Check exercises.
   • Labeling points with a value that is 1 less than the correct value, which may indicate a student is counting 0 when they count intervals from 0.
   • Not including a negative sign , indicating a lack of understanding that the values to the left of 0 are negative values.

4. **Next Steps** Assign the practice exercises to students who show understanding. For students who need more support, provide tutoring using the alternate teaching strategy.

Additional Teaching Resource
Online Transition Guide with Reteach and Extra Practice worksheets from previous grade levels

ALTERNATE INTERVENTION STRATEGY

Materials: several decks of playing cards TRT7 (Negative Number Lines)

Strategy: Use playing cards to practice graphing numbers on a number line.

1. Have students work in pairs. Give each pair of students a deck of playing cards and ask them to remove all the face cards (jacks, queens, kings, and jokers).

2. Explain that the value of each card is the number on the face of the card. The ace has a value of 1. If the card is red (hearts or diamonds), the number is a negative number. If the card is black (clubs or spades), the card is a positive number. For example, the 8 of hearts has a value of −8.

3. Draw the number line shown below on the board.

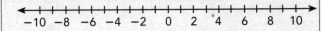

4. Have each student draw a card from his or her deck and place a dot on the number line where that number should be. Then place the card in the discard pile. Partners should check each other's answers.

5. Point out to students that sometimes there may be 2 dots at the same location on the number line, for instance, for the 5 of hearts and 5 of diamonds.

6. Have students continue this exercise until each student has graphed 5 numbers.

Represent Negative Numbers on a Number Line

Example

Locate −5 on the number line.

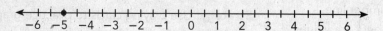

STEP 1 Locate 0. Negative numbers are to the left of 0 on the number line.

STEP 2 Count 5 to the left of 0 to locate −5.

✓ Quick Check

Identify the number that each indicated point represents.

1

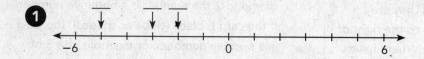

2

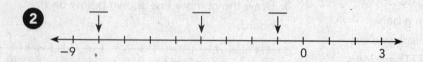

3

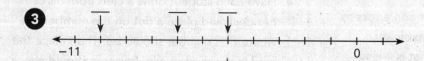

Practice on Your Own

Identify the number that each indicated point represents.

4

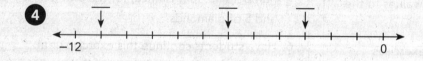

5

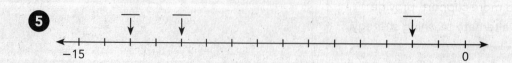

6

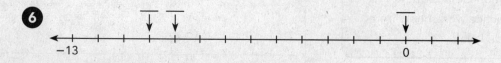

Identify the Absolute Value of a Number

TEACHING STRATEGY

1. **Vocabulary** Make sure students understand the meaning of the term *distance*. Direct students to the number line in Example 1. **Ask** What is the distance between −2 and 0? [2] Direct students to the number line in Example 2. **Ask** What is the distance between −5 and 2? [7]

2. **Teach** Review the information at the top of the student page. Work though Example 1 with students. Direct them to the number line. **Ask** As you measure the distance from 3 to 0, how many jumps do you make from unit to unit? [3] What direction do you jump? [to the left] If you measure the distance from 0 to 3, how many jumps do you make from unit to unit? [3] What direction do you jump? [to the right] Point out that distance is always positive. Then work though Example 2 with students. Write $|n| = -2$ on the board. **Ask** Can that statement ever be true? [No.] Why not? [The absolute value of a nonzero number is always a positive value.]

3. **Quick Check** Look for this common error as students solve the Quick Check exercises.
   - Writing negative absolute values for positive numbers, indicating that the student mistakenly believes the absolute value of a number is the opposite of that number.

4. **Next Steps** Assign the practice exercises to students who show understanding. For students who need more support, provide tutoring using the alternate teaching strategy.

Additional Teaching Resource
Online Transition Guide with Reteach and Extra Practice worksheets from previous grade levels

ALTERNATE INTERVENTION STRATEGY

Materials: scrap paper, TRT7 (Number Lines)

Strategy: Practice identifying absolute values by using a table that compares the distance from 0 of pairs of opposite numbers.

1. Draw the table below on the board. Have students copy it on scrap paper.

Negative Value	Distance from 0	Positive Value
−1		1
−2		2
−3		3
−4		4
−5		5

2. Remind students that the absolute value of a number is the distance on a number line between that number and zero. Tell students that they are going to complete the center column by measuring the distance along a number line between the given values and zero.

3. Distribute blank number lines. Instruct students to label their number lines in whole-unit intervals from −5 to 5.

4. For each of the values in the table, instruct students to count the number of jumps (the distance) between that value and zero. Encourage students to make conjectures about the relationship between $|-n|$ and $|n|$. [They are equal.]

5. After students have completed the table, write several numbers less than −5 and several numbers greater than 5 on the board. Ask students to identify the absolute value for each number without using a number line.

Name _____ Date _____

Identify the Absolute Value of a Number

The absolute value of a number is the distance between that number and zero on a number line.

The absolute value of any nonzero number is always positive.

Example 1 **Absolute Value of a Positive Number**

$|3|$ is read as "the absolute value of 3."

$|3|$ means the distance between 3 and 0 on a number line.

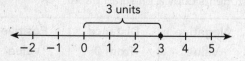

3 is 3 units away from 0.

So, its absolute value is 3.

$|3| = 3$

Example 2 **Absolute Value of a Negative Number**

$|-3|$ is read as "the absolute value of -3."

$|-3|$ means the distance between -3 and 0 on a number line.

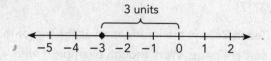

-3 is 3 units away from 0.

So, its absolute value is 3.

$|-3| = 3$

✔ Quick Check

Use the symbol || to write the absolute values of the following numbers.

1 2 _____

2 -6 _____

3 -7 _____

Practice on Your Own

Use the symbol || to write the absolute values of the following numbers.

4 1 _____

5 -5 _____

6 -4 _____

7 8 _____

8 9 _____

9 6 _____

10 -9 _____

11 12 _____

12 -8 _____

13 11 _____

14 -15 _____

15 0 _____

Find the Perimeter of a Polygon

TEACHING STRATEGY

1. **Vocabulary** Make sure students understand the terms *perimeter, polygon, regular polygon, square, trapezoid, parallelogram, pentagon,* and *equilateral triangle.* To help students with each type of polygon, have them make a chart with the name of the figure and its properties. As examples, for regular polygon, the property listed is "all identical sides;" for "square," the property listed is "4 identical sides;" and so on. Instruct students to refer to the chart they have created as they complete the worksheet.

2. **Teach** Introduce the idea of perimeter of a polygon. **Ask** What must you do first to find the perimeter of a polygon? [Identify all the sides of the polygon.] What do you do next? [Write an equation for the perimeter.] Tell students that they must substitute the length of each side into the equation and then find the sum. **Ask** Is there an easier way to find the perimeter of a regular polygon? [Yes, you can multiply the side length by the number of sides.]

3. **Quick Check** Look for these common errors as students solve the Quick Check exercises.
   - Omitting a side length of a polygon thereby finding an incorrect perimeter.
   - Not including units in answers, indicating confusion about the idea of perimeter.

4. **Next Steps** Assign the practice exercises to students who show understanding. For students who need more support, provide tutoring using the alternate teaching strategy.

Additional Teaching Resource
Online Transition Guide with Reteach and Extra Practice worksheets from previous grade levels

ALTERNATE INTERVENTION STRATEGY

Materials: multiple copies of the game cards below

Strategy: Use formulas to find perimeters of polygons.

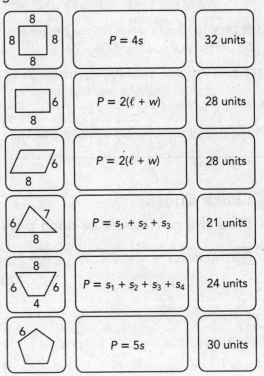

1. Distribute decks of game cards to pairs of students. Tell students they are going to play Go Fish. Have students shuffle the deck and deal each student 4 cards. The remaining cards in their deck are placed face down between students.

2. The goal of the game is to get the most sets of three matching cards: one with a figure, one with the formula for finding its perimeter, and one with the correct perimeter for that figure.

3. Students take turns asking their partner for a specific card (a regular pentagon, $P = 5s$, 30 units). If the partner has the card, he or she surrenders it and the original student asks for another card. If the partner does not have the card requested, the original student draws a card from the pile, and the partner asks for a card. Play continues until all cards have been drawn and correctly matched.

Find the Perimeter of a Polygon

Example

The perimeter of a polygon is the distance around the polygon. Figure *WXYZ* is a trapezoid. Find its perimeter.

STEP 1 Identify the sides of the polygon. Trapezoid *WXYZ* has 4 sides: $\overline{WX}$, $\overline{XY}$, $\overline{YZ}$, and $\overline{ZW}$.

STEP 2 Write an equation for the perimeter.
$P = WX + XY + YZ + ZW$

STEP 3 Substitute the value for the length of each side into the equation and find the sum.
$P = 4 + 6 + 8 + 6 = 24$

The perimeter of trapezoid *WXYZ* is 24 inches, or 24 in.

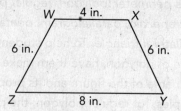

✔ Quick Check
Find the perimeter of each polygon.

1 Figure *RST* is an equilateral triangle.

3 in.

P = _____

2 Figure *EFGH* is a rectangle.

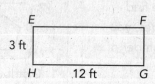

3 ft

12 ft

P = _____

3 Figure *LMNOP* is a regular pentagon.

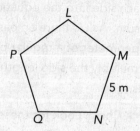

5 m

P = _____

Practice on Your Own
Find the perimeter of each polygon.

1 Figure *ABCD* is a square.

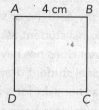

A   4 cm   B

P = _____

2 Figure *RSTU* is a parallelogram.

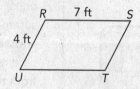

R   7 ft   S

4 ft

P = _____

3 Figure *JKLM* is a trapezoid.

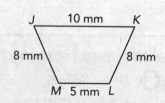

J   10 mm   K

8 mm   8 mm

M 5 mm L

P = _____

Find the Area of a Rectangle Using a Formula

TEACHING STRATEGY

1. **Vocabulary** Make sure students understand the terms *length*, *width*, and *area*, as well as how the three terms are related. **Ask** What do we call the measurement of a longer side of a rectangle? [its length] What do we call the measurement of a shorter side of a rectangle? [its width] Point out that length and width are linear dimensions, so they are measured in simple linear units, such as inches, feet, centimeters, or meters. Explain that area is the product of two linear dimensions, so it is measured in square units, such as square inches, square feet, square centimeters, or square meters. Show students how to abbreviate those units.

2. **Teach** Direct students to the formula in Step 1. **Ask** What is the length of the rectangle? [10 cm] What is the width of the rectangle? [5 cm] When we substitute those values into the formula, what equation do we get? [$A = 10 \cdot 5$] Direct students to the equation in Step 2. **Ask** What is the unit for area in this example? [square centimeters] What is the area of the rectangle? [50 square centimeters]

3. **Quick Check** Look for these common errors as students solve the Quick Check exercises.
   - Using the formula for perimeter rather than area.
   - Giving answers with linear units instead of square units.

4. **Next Steps** Assign the practice exercises to students who show understanding. For students who need more support, provide tutoring using the alternate teaching strategy.

Additional Teaching Resource
Online Transition Guide with Reteach and Extra Practice worksheets from previous grade levels

ALTERNATE INTERVENTION STRATEGY

Materials: TRT12 (Graph Paper)

Strategy: Use a unit grid to develop the formula for the area of a rectangle.

1. Remind students that the area of a figure is the amount of surface it covers. Area can be determined by counting the number of unit squares covered by a figure.

2. Distribute graph paper. Across the top of the paper, have students label the first ten rows 1–10. Then, along the left side of the paper, have them label the first ten columns 1–10.

	1	2	3	4	5	6	7	8	9	10
1										
2										
3										
4										
5										
6										
7										
8										
9										
10										

Give students various side length pairs. For example, say "The length of the rectangle is 5 and the width is 7." Have students draw on the grid a rectangle with those measurements. Also have them label the two dimensions.

3. Write $A = \ell \cdot w$. Below it, write $A = 5 \cdot 7$. **Ask** How many squares are covered by the rectangle? [35] What is the area of the rectangle? [35 square units]. Write $A = 5 \cdot 7 = 35$ square units.

4. Repeat the activity with several other dimension pairs. Each time, demonstrate how the formula for the area of a rectangle relates to the dimensions of the rectangle. Then show how the product of those dimensions is equal to the number of squares the rectangle covers.

Find the Area of a Rectangle Using a Formula

Name _____ Date _____

Find the area of the rectangle at right.

STEP 1 Write the formula for the area of a rectangle.

$Area = length \cdot width$ or $A = \ell w$

STEP 2 Substitute the length of the longer side, 10, for ℓ in the formula. Substitute the length of the shorter side, 5, for w.

$A = 10 \cdot 5$

STEP 3 Multiply.

$A = 10 \cdot 5 = 50$ The area of the rectangle is 50 square centimeters, or 50 cm².

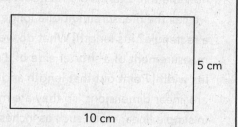

✔ Quick Check

Find the area of each rectangle.

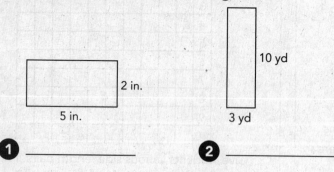

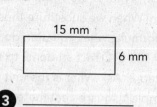

1 _____

2 _____

3 _____

Practice on Your Own

Find the area of each rectangle.

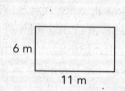

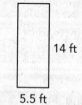

4 _____

5 _____

Solve.

6 The length of a rectangle is 18.3 yards and its width is 9 yards.

Find the area of the rectangle. _____

Find the Area of a Square Using a Formula

TEACHING STRATEGY

1. **Vocabulary** Make sure students understand the term *square*. Point out that a square is a special type of rectangle with four sides that are all the same length. **Ask** How else is the term square used in mathematics? [a square of a number, square roots] **Ask** What does it mean to "square" a number? [to multiply a number by itself]

2. **Teach** Remind students that area is measured in unit squares and that a unit square has side lengths that measure 1 unit and an area that measures 1 square unit. Direct students to the figure of the square in the example. Help them visualize the figure as a 7 × 7 grid of unit squares. **Ask** If each unit square is a square foot, how many unit squares would run across the top side of the square? [7] **Ask** How many unit squares would run down the left side? [7] Have students create a grid of unit squares over the figures. **Ask** How many unit squares are covered a square that is 7 by 7? [49] Do you need 2 side lengths to find the area of a square? [No, just one side length, which then can be squared to find the area.]

3. **Quick Check** Look for these common errors as students solve the Quick Check exercises.
   - Mistakenly using the formula for perimeter instead of area.
   - Confusing the use of the exponent 2 with "multiply by 2."
   - Forgetting to square the units in the answers.

4. **Next Steps** Assign the practice exercises to students who show understanding. For students who need more support, provide tutoring using the alternate teaching strategy.

Additional Teaching Resource
Online Transition Guide with Reteach and Extra Practice worksheets from previous grade levels

ALTERNATE INTERVENTION STRATEGY

Materials: dot paper

Strategy: Use dot paper to develop the formula for the area of a square.

1. Remind students that the number of dots in an array is equal to the product of the number of dots in each row and the number of dots in each column.

2. Distribute dot paper. Have students draw a horizontal line that connects 5 dots. From the end of that line, have them draw a vertical line down that connects 5 dots. Then have students draw two more sides to complete the square.

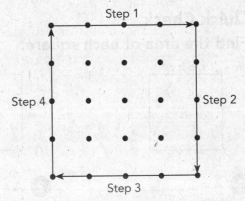

Ask How many dots are in each row? [5] How many dots are in each column? [5] Label the dimensions of the square. Write $A = \ell^2$. Below it, write $A = 5^2 = 5 \cdot 5$. **Ask** How many dots are connected and enclosed by the square? [25 dots] What is the area of the square? [25 square units] Write $A = 5^2 = 5 \cdot 5 = 25$ square units.

4. If necessary, repeat the activity with squares that have other side lengths. Each time, demonstrate how the formula for the area of a square relates to the number of dots in each row and column of the array. Then show how the product of the dimensions is equal to the total number of dots in the array.

Name _____ Date _____

Find the Area of a Square Using a Formula

Example

Find the area of a square: Area = length × length, or $A = \ell^2$.

STEP 1 Write the formula for the area of a square.

Area = length · width   or $A = \ell^2$

STEP 2 Substitute the value for the length into the formula.

$A = 7^2$ Remember, when you "square" a number, you multiply it by itself.

STEP 3 Multiply.

$A = 7 \times 7 = 49$ The area of the square is 49 square feet, or 49 ft².

7 ft

✔ Quick Check
Find the area of each square.

6 ft

10 m

12 cm

1 A = _____

2 A = _____

3 A = _____

Practice on Your Own
Find the area of each square.

25 cm

9.5 in.

4 A = _____

5 A = _____

Solve.

6 A side length of a square is 21 millimeters. Find the area of the square.

_____

7 A side length of a square is 14.6 feet. Find the area of the square.

_____

Identify Trapezoids, Parallelograms, and Rhombuses

G SKILL 41

TEACHING STRATEGY

1. **Vocabulary** Make sure students understand the term *parallel*. **Ask** What are parallel lines? [lines that lie in the same plane and never intersect] What can you say about the directions parallel lines point in? [They point in the same direction.] What can you say about the distance between two parallel lines? [Along the entire length of the lines, the distance remains the same.]

2. **Teach** Before reviewing the properties, make sure students are familiar with the symbols used to indicate parallelism and congruency. Direct students to the figure in Example 1. **Ask** What do the single tick marks, the short lines drawn across sides $\overline{AB}$ and $\overline{DC}$, mean? [$\overline{AB}$ and $\overline{DC}$ are the same length.] What do the double tick marks on sides $\overline{AD}$ and $\overline{BC}$ mean? [$\overline{AD}$ and $\overline{BC}$ are the same length.] What do the single arrows along sides $\overline{AD}$ and $\overline{BC}$ mean? [$\overline{AD}$ and $\overline{BC}$ are parallel.] What do the double arrows along sides $\overline{AB}$ and $\overline{DC}$ mean? [$\overline{AB}$ and $\overline{DC}$ are parallel.]

3. **Quick Check** Look for these common errors as students solve the Quick Check exercises.
   - Identifying adjacent sides of a rhombus as parallel, indicating confusion between marks showing parallelism and marks showing congruency.
   - Identifying rhombuses as parallelograms, indicating a lack of understanding that all four sides of a rhombus are the same length.

4. **Next Steps** Assign the practice exercises to students who show understanding. For students who need more support, provide tutoring using the alternate teaching strategy.

Additional Teaching Resource

🖱 Online Transition Guide with Reteach and Extra Practice worksheets from previous grade levels

ALTERNATE INTERVENTION STRATEGY

Materials: index cards

Strategy: Use a matching game to help learn the properties of parallelograms, trapezoids, and rhombuses. Students play in pairs.

1. Create two sets of game cards for each pair: a set of six figure cards that includes two of each type, and a set of property cards that includes two statements about parallelism and two about congruence.

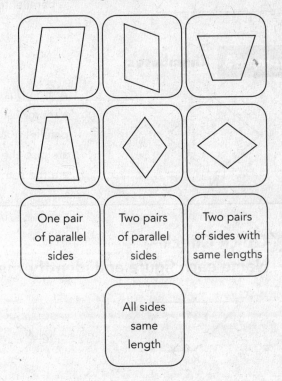

2. One student draws a "figure" card. The partner matches the correct property card(s) to the figure, then writes the property or properties on the back of the card along with the name of the figure. Students alternate until all six figures have been identified.

3. You may want to time the game. If so, the first pair of students to correctly identify all six figures and their properties is the winner.

Name _____ Date _____

Identify Trapezoids, Parallelograms, and Rhombuses

Example 1 **Parallelograms** ─────────────

A parallelogram has two pairs of parallel sides. Opposite sides are also the same length. In parallelogram ABCD, $\overline{AB}$ is parallel to $\overline{DC}$, and $\overline{AD}$ is parallel to $\overline{BC}$. $\overline{AB}$ is the same length as $\overline{DC}$, and $\overline{AD}$ is the same length as $\overline{BC}$.

Example 2 **Trapezoids**

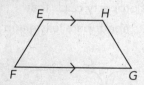

A trapezoid has only one pair of parallel sides. In trapezoid EFGH, $\overline{EF}$ is parallel to $\overline{FG}$.

Example 3 **Rhombuses**

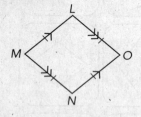

A rhombus is a special type of parallelogram. Like all parallelograms, a rhombus has two pairs of parallel sides. In rhombus LMNO, $\overline{LO}$ is parallel to $\overline{MN}$, and $\overline{LM}$ is parallel to $\overline{ON}$. In a rhombus, all four sides are also the same length. In rhombus LMNO, $\overline{LO}$, $\overline{ON}$, $\overline{NM}$, and $\overline{ML}$ are the same length.

☑ Quick Check

Name each figure and identify the pairs of parallel sides.

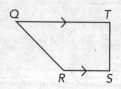   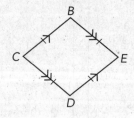   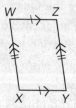

1 _____   **2** _____   **3** _____

Practice on Your Own

Name each figure and identify the pairs of parallel sides.

   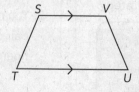   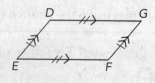

4 _____   **5** _____   **6** _____

Add Decimals

TEACHING STRATEGY

1. **Vocabulary** Make sure students understand the term *regroup*. **Ask** How do you regroup when you find the sum of 9 + 9? [9 + 9 is equal to 18 ones. You regroup 10 ones at 1 ten, so the result is 1 ten and 8 ones.]

2. **Teach** Remind students that when adding decimals, it is necessary to first rewrite the problem vertically in order to align the decimal points. It is also helpful to annex zeros as placeholders so that all the numbers have the same number of digits after the decimal point. Explain that all the same rules apply to working with decimals as they do to working with whole numbers. For example, if the sum of the digits in any given column (tens, ones, tenths, hundredths, etc.) is greater than 9, the sum must be regrouped. Work through the example with students. **Ask** In Step 1, why should you write a zero at the end of 2.88? [Possible answer: The zero is a placeholder. It helps you align the digits in each number correctly.] In Step 4, why do you have to regroup? [Possible answer: The sum of 5 tenths and 8 tenths is 13 tenths. So you need to regroup the sum as 1 one and 3 tenths.]

3. **Quick Check** Look for these common errors as students solve the Quick Check exercises.
   - Misaligning the decimal points when writing a problem vertically, indicating confusion about place value.
   - Incorrectly regrouping and/or renaming when adding.

4. **Next Steps** Assign the practice exercises to students who show understanding. For students who need more support, provide tutoring using the alternate teaching strategy.

Additional Teaching Resource
Online Transition Guide with Reteach and Extra Practice worksheets from previous grade levels

ALTERNATE INTERVENTION STRATEGY

Materials: place-value charts

Strategy: Use a place-value chart to add decimals.

1. Display a place-value chart or distribute charts to students. You may wish to make place-value charts for the purposes of this activity. The charts should have columns for the tens place through the thousandths place.

2. Write 13.09 + 1.825 on the board.

3. Have students write the problem vertically in their charts.
   - Work with students to find the sum of the numbers in each column.
   - Remind students that they must regroup when adding the hundredths and rename 10 hundredths as 1 tenth.

t e n s	o n e s	.	t e n t h s	h u n d r e d t h s	t h o u s a n d t h s
			1		
1	3	.	0	9	0
+ 1	1	.	8	2	5
1	4	.	9	1	5

4. Provide more examples for students to solve using their place-value charts.

5. Once students become comfortable with adding decimals on their charts, have them work through additional examples without using the charts.

Add Decimals

Example

Find the value of 0.512 + 2.88.

STEP 1 Rewrite the problem vertically. Carefully align the decimal points. Write a zero at the end of 2.88 as a placeholder.

$$\begin{array}{r} 0.512 \\ + 2.880 \\ \hline \end{array}$$

STEP 2 Start from the right side. Add the digits in the thousandths place.

2 thousandths + 0 thousandths = 2 thousandths

$$\begin{array}{r} 0.512 \\ + 2.880 \\ \hline 2 \end{array}$$

STEP 3 Add the digits in the hundredths place.

1 hundredth + 8 hundredths = 9 hundredths

$$\begin{array}{r} 0.512 \\ + 2.880 \\ \hline 92 \end{array}$$

STEP 4 Add the digits in the tens place. Because the sum 13 is > 9, regroup the tenths.

5 tenths + 8 tenths = 1 one 3 tenths

$$\begin{array}{r} \overset{1}{0}.512 \\ + 2.880 \\ \hline 392 \end{array}$$

STEP 5 Place the decimal point in the answer. Add the digits in the ones place.

1 one + 0 ones + 2 ones = 3 ones

$$\begin{array}{r} \overset{1}{0}.512 \\ + 2.880 \\ \hline 3.392 \end{array}$$

✔ Quick Check
Add.

1 8.7 + 12.23

2 43.407 + 3.91

3 0.82 + 4.225

Practice on Your Own
Add.

4 15.62 + 0.808

5 10.05 + 5.55

6 42.62 + 9.7

7 0.028 + 18.99

8 4.2 + 2.05

9 8.1 + 16.9

Subtract Decimals

TEACHING STRATEGY

1. **Vocabulary** Make sure students understand the term *regroup*. **Ask** When do you need to regroup when subtracting numbers? [when you are trying to subtract a greater digit from a lesser digit.]

2. **Teach** Explain to students that, just as when adding decimals, it is necessary to first rewrite a subtraction problem with decimals in vertical format in order to align the decimal points. Remind them to annex zeros as placeholders to avoid confusion when subtracting the digits in each column. If necessary, review how to regroup and rename when subtracting numbers. Work through the Example with students. **Ask** In Step 3, why do you need to regroup? [You cannot subtract 1 hundredth from 0 hundredths.] What are you regrouping? [You are regrouping 1 tenth as 10 hundredths.] Why must you cross out the 7 and rename it as 6? [You have regrouped 1 tenth in order to subtract the hundredths, so you must subtract 1 tenth from the 7 tenths.]

3. **Quick Check** Look for these common errors as students solve the Quick Check exercises.
   - Misaligning decimal points when writing problems vertically, indicating confusion over place value.
   - Incorrectly regrouping and/or renaming.

4. **Next Steps** Assign the practice exercises to students who show understanding. For students who need more support, provide tutoring using the alternate teaching strategy.

Additional Teaching Resource
Online Transition Guide with Reteach and Extra Practice worksheets from previous grade levels

ALTERNATE INTERVENTION STRATEGY

Materials: place-value charts

Strategy: Use a place-value chart to subtract decimals.

1. Display a place-value chart or distribute charts to students. You may wish to make place-value charts for the purposes of this activity. The charts should have columns for the tens place through the thousandths place.

2. Write $27.826 - 4.65$ on the board.

3. Have students write the problem vertically in their charts.
   - Work with students to find the difference of the numbers in each column.
   - Remind students that they must regroup when subtracting the hundredths, regrouping 7 tenths as 6 tenths and 10 hundredths, and changing 2 hundredths to 12 hundredths.

t e n s	o n e s	.	t e n t h s	h u n d r e d t h s	t h o u s a n d t h s
2	7	.	$\overset{7}{\cancel{8}}$	$\overset{12}{\cancel{2}}$	6
−	4	.	6	5	0
2	3	.	1	7	6

4. Provide more examples for students to solve using their place-value charts.

5. Once students become comfortable with adding decimals on their charts, have them work through additional examples without using the charts.

Subtract Decimals

Example

Find the value of 5.702 − 4.61.

STEP 1 Rewrite the problem vertically, aligning the decimal points.
Write a zero at the end of 4.61 as a placeholder.

$$\begin{array}{r} 5.702 \\ -\ 4.610 \\ \hline \end{array}$$

STEP 2 Start from the right side. Subtract the digits in the
thousandths place.
2 thousandths − 0 thousandths = 2 thousandths

$$\begin{array}{r} 5.702 \\ -\ 4.610 \\ \hline 2 \end{array}$$

STEP 3 Regroup 1 tenth as 10 hundredths. Subtract the digits in
the hundredths place.
10 hundredths − 1 hundredth = 9 hundredths

$$\begin{array}{r} {}^{6\ 10}\ \\ 5.7\cancel{0}2 \\ -\ 4.610 \\ \hline 92 \end{array}$$

STEP 4 Subtract the digits in the tens place.
6 tenths − 6 tenths = 0 tenths

$$\begin{array}{r} {}^{6\ 10}\ \\ 5.7\cancel{0}2 \\ -\ 4.610 \\ \hline 092 \end{array}$$

STEP 5 Place the decimal point in the answer. Subtract the digits in
the ones place.
5 ones − 4 ones = 1 ones

$$\begin{array}{r} {}^{6\ 10}\ \\ 5.7\cancel{0}2 \\ -\ 4.610 \\ \hline 1.092 \end{array}$$

☑ Quick Check
Subtract.

1 30.5 − 2.4

2 19.25 − 11.05

3 22.4 − 0.05

Practice on Your Own
Subtract.

4 1.6 − 0.99

5 43.6 − 29.57

6 3.16 − 0.28

7 11 − 6.43

8 67.48 − 66.86

9 15.78 − 3.3

Multiply Decimals

TEACHING STRATEGY

1. **Vocabulary** Make sure students understand the term *regroup* in the context of multiplication. **Ask** When do you need to regroup when multiplying numbers? [You need to regroup when the product of 2 digits is 10 or greater. You have to regroup the tens to the next higher place value. Then you need to add that regrouped value to the product of the digits in the next higher place value.]

2. **Teach** Remind students that multiplying decimals is just like multiplying whole numbers. The only difference is having to place the decimal point. Review the steps of the Example with students. **Ask** Why is it not necessary to line up the decimal points in each factor when rewriting the problem? [Possible answer: The product must have the same number of decimal places as the total number of decimal places in both factors. You can multiply the numbers like you would any two whole numbers and place the decimal point in the product as a last step.] You may also want to remind students about multiplying decimals by powers of 10. Tell students they can count the number of zeros in the power of 10. Then move the decimal point in the other factor to the right the same number of places as the number of zeros they counted.

3. **Quick Check** Look for this common error as students solve the Quick Check exercises.
   - Misplacing the decimal point in the final product, indicating a lack of understanding of place value.

4. **Next Steps** Assign the practice exercises to students who show understanding. For students who need more support, provide tutoring using the alternate teaching strategy.

Additional Teaching Resource

Online Transition Guide with Reteach and Extra Practice worksheets from previous grade levels

ALTERNATE INTERVENTION STRATEGY

Materials: multiple copies of the maze shown below

Strategy: Practice multiplying decimals with partners.

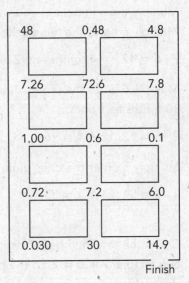

48	0.48	4.8
7.26	72.6	7.8
1.00	0.6	0.1
0.72	7.2	6.0
0.030	30	14.9

Finish

1. Review the steps for multiplying decimals. If necessary, review the intervention strategies for multiplying whole numbers.

2. Have students work in pairs. Give each pair a copy of the maze.

3. Tell students they are going to work their way through the maze by finding the correct product to each of the problems you write on the board. To get through the maze, students will move from one correct answer to another until they reach the area marked "Finish."

Problems: a. Start. 0.12 · 40 [4.8]
b. 1.3 * 6 [7.8]
c. 12.1 · 6 [72.6]
d. 12 · 0.05 [0.6]
e. 4 · 0.25 [1.00]
f. 0.09 · 8 [0.72]
g. 0.006 · 5 [0.030]
h. 1.5 · 20 [30]
i. 2.98 · 5 [14.9]

Multiply Decimals

Example

Find the value of 9.27 · 6.

STEP 1 Rewrite the problem vertically. Do not align digits by place value.

$$\begin{array}{r} 9.27 \\ \times\ \ 6 \\ \hline \end{array}$$

STEP 2 Multiply the numbers as you would multiply whole numbers.
Multiply 6 times the hundredths digit, 7. Regroup 40 hundredths as 4 tenths.

$7 \cdot 6 = 42$ 4 tenths and 2 hundredths

$$\begin{array}{r} \overset{4}{9}.27 \\ \times\ \ 6 \\ \hline 2 \end{array}$$

STEP 3 Multiply 6 times the tenths digit, 2. Add the regrouped 4 tenths. Regroup
10 tenths as 1 one.

$2 \cdot 6 = 12; 12 + 4 = 16$ 1 one and 6 tenths

$$\begin{array}{r} \overset{1\ 4}{9}.27 \\ \times\ \ 6 \\ \hline 62 \end{array}$$

STEP 4 Multiply 6 times the ones digit, 9. Add the regrouped 1 one.

$9 \cdot 6 = 54; 54 + 1 = 55$

$$\begin{array}{r} \overset{1\ 4}{9}.27 \\ \times\ \ 6 \\ \hline 55.62 \end{array}$$

STEP 5 Count the total number of digits to the right of the decimal point in the
two factors. $2 + 0 = 2$, so the product must have 2 digits to the right of the
decimal point.

$$\begin{array}{r} \overset{1\ 4}{9}.27 \\ \times\ \ 6 \\ \hline 55.62 \end{array}$$

☑ Quick Check
Multiply.

1 5 · 0.9

2 4.23 · 9

3 0.865 · 3

_____   _____   _____

Practice on Your Own
Multiply.

4 7 · 2.08

5 10.75 · 2

6 1.035 · 4

_____   _____   _____

7 0.028 · 3

8 6 · 5.41

9 3.99 · 7

_____   _____   _____

Divide Decimals

TEACHING STRATEGY

1. **Vocabulary** Review with students the terms *dividend*, *divisor*, and *quotient*. Point out that when written horizontally, the dividend is the first term, the divisor is the second term, and the quotient is the final answer. **Ask** When using long division, which term is written inside the box? [the dividend] Which term is written in front of the box? [the divisor]

2. **Teach** Remind students that dividing decimals is similar to dividing whole numbers, with an extra first step: placing the decimal point in the quotient before you begin to divide. Review the Example, emphasizing that it is absolutely necessary to write the decimal point in the quotient directly above the decimal point in the dividend. **Ask** Why can you ignore the decimal point in the dividend when you begin dividing? [Possible answer: You have already placed the decimal point in the correct spot in the quotient. So you can divide as you would with whole numbers because your answer will already be in the form of a decimal.]

3. **Quick Check** Look for this common error as students solve the Quick Check exercises.
   - Misplacing or forgetting to place the decimal point in the quotient.
   This error indicates a lack of understanding of place value.

4. **Next Steps** Assign the practice exercises to students who show understanding. For students who need more support, provide tutoring using the alternate teaching strategy.

Additional Teaching Resource
🖱 Online Transition Guide with Reteach and Extra Practice worksheets from previous grade levels

ALTERNATE INTERVENTION STRATEGY

Materials: multiple copies of the cards shown below

Strategy: Study the steps in the process of subtracting decimals.

1. Using index cards, create multiple sets of the 12 cards shown below.

$45.9 \div 3$	$72.6 \div 6$	$0.84 \div 4$
$0.35 \div 7$	$12.5 \div 5$	$2.4 \div 6$
$5.52 \div 12$	$1.54 \div 7$	$0.256 \div 4$
$0.825 \div 5$	$0.016 \div 4$	$0.81 \div 9$

2. Have students work in pairs. Give each pair of students a set of game cards and instruct them to shuffle the cards. With the cards face down, students should take turns selecting one card from the deck until each students has 6 cards.

3. Instruct students to turn their cards over and rewrite the problems on the back of each card for long division. Students also should place the decimal point in each quotient. They should NOT solve the problems. When both students in each pair have rewritten all of their problems, they should trade cards and check each other's work for any errors.

4. Instruct students to work together to solve the problems.

Answers (in order from left to right and top to bottom): 15.3, 12.1, 0.21, 0.05, 2.5, 0.4, 0.46, 0.22, 0.064, 0.165, 0.004, 0.09

Divide Decimals

Name _____ Date _____

Example

Find the value of 7.68 ÷ 8.

STEP 1 Rewrite the problem for long division.

$$8 \overline{)7.68}$$

STEP 2 Place a decimal point in the quotient directly above the decimal point in the dividend.

$$8 \overline{)7.68}$$

STEP 3 Divide the numbers as you would divide whole numbers, looking at each digit from left to right. You cannot divide 7 ones by 8. Write a zero in the quotient above the 7.

$$\begin{array}{r} 0. \\ 8 \overline{)7.68} \end{array}$$

STEP 4 Move to the next place to the right and divide.

76 tenths ÷ 8 = 9 tenths R 4 tenths

$$\begin{array}{r} 0.9 \\ 8 \overline{)7.68} \\ -7\,2 \\ \hline 4 \end{array}$$

STEP 5 Bring down the 8 hundredths and continue dividing.

48 hundredths ÷ 8 = 6 hundredths

So, 7.68 ÷ 8 = 0.96.

$$\begin{array}{r} 0.96 \\ 8 \overline{)7.68} \\ -7\,2\downarrow \\ \hline 48 \\ -48 \\ \hline 0 \end{array}$$

✔ Quick Check

Divide.

1 11.2 ÷ 7

2 8.12 ÷ 4

3 0.85 ÷ 5

_____

Practice on Your Own
Divide.

4 7.08 ÷ 2

5 4.32 ÷ 6

6 0.508 ÷ 4

_____

7 22.5 ÷ 9

8 7.47 ÷ 3

9 0.528 ÷ 6

_____

Round Numbers to the Nearest Whole Number

TEACHING STRATEGY

1. **Vocabulary** Make sure students understand the phrase *rounding to the nearest whole number.* **Ask** If you're rounding a number to the nearest whole number, what place are you rounding to? [the ones place]

2. **Teach** Work through the Examples with students, reviewing the steps in the rounding process. **Ask** What is the first step in rounding a number? [Possible answer: Find the place you want to round to.] What is the second step in rounding? [Possible answer: Look at the first digit to the right of the place you're rounding to.] If you are rounding to the nearest whole number, what place do you need to look at? [the tenths place] In your own words, explain how to round a number to the nearest whole number. [Possible answer: Look at the digit in the tenths place. If the digit is less than 5, the digit in the ones place does not change. If the digit is 5 or greater, the digit in the ones place increases by 1.]

3. **Quick Check** Look for this common error as students solve the Quick Check exercises.
   • Looking at the last digit in a number instead of the digit to the right of the rounding place to decide how to round.

   This error indicates a lack of understanding of place value.

4. **Next Steps** Assign the practice exercises to students who show understanding. For students who need more support, provide tutoring using the alternate teaching strategy.

Additional Teaching Resource

 Online Transition Guide with Reteach and Extra Practice worksheets from previous grade levels

ALTERNATE INTERVENTION STRATEGY

Materials: TRT1 (Number Lines)

Strategy: Use a number line to round decimals to the nearest whole number.

1. Tell students they are going to round 4.6 to the nearest whole number using a number line.

2. Draw a number line on the board like the one shown below. Place a point on the number line to identify 4.6.

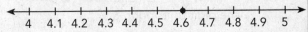

4   4.1 4.2 4.3 4.4 4.5 4.6 4.7 4.8 4.9 5

3. Remind students they need to round 4.6 to the nearest whole number. **Ask** What two whole numbers is 4.6 between? [4 and 5]

4. Have students compare the distance from 4.6 to 4 and its distance from 5. **Ask** Which whole number is 4.6 nearer to on the number line—4 or 5? [4.6 is closer to 5.] Therefore, 4.6 rounded to the nearest whole number is 5.

5. Repeat the process with 7.5. **Ask** What whole number is 7.5 closer to on the number line—7 or 8? [7.5 is halfway between 7 and 8, so it is the same distance from both whole numbers.]

6. Explain to students that when a number lies halfway between two whole numbers, it is rounded to the greater whole number, the whole number to the right.

7. Provide students with additional examples and have them use their own number lines to round the numbers to the nearest whole number. Once students feel comfortable with using a number line to round, work with them to develop a set of rules for rounding based on generalizations they can make about a number's position on the number line.

Name _____ Date _____

Round Numbers to the Nearest Whole Number

Round decimals the same way you round whole numbers.

STEP 1 Identify the digit to round to. When rounding to the nearest whole number, round to ones.

STEP 2 Look at the digit to the right of the rounding digit. When rounding to ones, look at the tenths.
- If the tenths digit is 5 or greater, "round up." Add 1 to the digit in the ones place.
- If the tenths digit is less than 5, "round down." Do not change the digit in the ones place.

STEP 3 Delete all the digits to the right of the rounding digit.

Example 1 Next digit ≥ 5 ───────

Round 14.62 to the nearest whole number.

14.<u>6</u>2   4 is in the rounding place, ones. Look at the digit to its right, 6.

15.<u>6</u>2   6 > 5, so "round up" the 4 in the ones place to 5. Then delete all the digits to its right.

14.62 rounded to the nearest whole number is 15.

Example 2 Next digit < 5 ───────

Round 9.29 to the nearest whole number.

9.<u>2</u>8   9 is in the rounding place, ones. Look at the digit to its right, 2.

9.<u>2</u>8   2 < 5, so "round down." Do not change the 9 in the ones place. Delete all the digits to its right.

9.28 rounded to the nearest whole number is 9.

✓ Quick Check
Round to the nearest whole number.

1 30.5

2 43.25

3 22.35

_____   _____   _____

Practice on Your Own
Round to the nearest whole number.

4 6.95

5 29.57

6 3.16

_____   _____   _____

7 31.43

8 17.85

9 65.78

_____   _____   _____

Round Numbers to the Nearest Tenth

TEACHING STRATEGY

1. **Vocabulary** Make sure students understand the phrase *rounding to the nearest tenth*. **Ask** If you're rounding a number to the nearest tenth, how many decimal places will be in your answer? [1 decimal place: tenths]

2. **Teach** Work through the Examples with students, reviewing the steps in the rounding process. **Ask** What is the first step in rounding a number? [Possible answer: Find the place you want to round to.] What is the second step in rounding? [Possible answer: Look at the first digit to the right of the place you're rounding to.] If you are rounding to the nearest tenth, what place do you need to look at? [The hundredths place] Point out that when a decimal contains a 9 in the tenths place and is followed by a hundredths digit greater than or equal to 5, the 9 tenths will round up to 10 ones. Instruct students to write a zero in the tenths place to indicate that the number was rounded to the correct place. For example: 4.98 rounded to the nearest tenth is 5.0.

3. **Quick Check** Look for these common errors as students solve the Quick Check exercises.
   - Looking at the value of the tenths digit to determine whether to round up or down.
   - Keeping the digits to the right of the rounding place after rounding (e.g., thinking that 1.57 rounds to 1.67).

   These errors indicate a lack of understanding of place value and the purpose of estimation.

4. **Next Steps** Assign the practice exercises to students who show understanding. For students who need more support, provide tutoring using the alternate teaching strategy.

Additional Teaching Resource

 Online Transition Guide with Reteach and Extra Practice worksheets from previous grade levels

ALTERNATE INTERVENTION STRATEGY

Materials: place-value chart

Strategy: Use a place-value chart to round decimals to the nearest tenth.

1. Display a place-value chart showing tens to hundredths and review the place values with students.

t e n s	o n e s	.	t e n t h s	h u n d r e d t h s
2	3	.	4	5

2. Write the number 23.45 in the chart and tell students you want to round the number to the nearest tenth.

3. Review the steps for rounding a number with students. **Ask** What place is to the right of tenths? [hundredths] What digit is in the hundredths place? [5] Do I need to round the tenths digit up or down? Why? [Round up; when the digit is 5 or greater, round up.]

4. Work through a few additional examples with students. Then have students use their own place-value charts to round the numbers below. Suggest to students that they highlight the hundredths column in their charts to help them round the numbers correctly.

3.72 [3.7]	18.66 [18.7]	0.72 [0.7]
34.15 [34.2]	5.09 [5.1]	62.94 [62.9]

Round Numbers to the Nearest Tenth

Name _____ Date _____

Round decimals the same way you round whole numbers.

STEP 1 Identify the digit you are rounding to.

STEP 2 Look at the digit to the right of the rounding digit. When rounding to tenths, look at the hundredths digit.

- If the hundredths digit is 5 or greater, "round up." Add 1 to the digit in the tenths place.
- If the hundredths digit is less than 5, "round down." Do not change the digit in the tenths place.

STEP 3 Delete all the digits to the right of the rounding digit.

Example 1 Next digit ≥ 5

Round 25.17 to the nearest tenth.

25.1**7**   1 is in the rounding place, tenths. Look at the digit to its right, 7.

25.2**7**   7 > 5, so "round up" the 1 in the tenths place to 2. Then delete all the digits to its right.

25.17 rounded to the nearest tenth is 25.2.

Example 2 Next digit < 5

Round 4.82 to the nearest tenth.

4.8**2**   8 is in the rounding place, tenths. Look at the digit to its right, 2.

4.8**2**   2 < 5, so "round down." Do not change the 8 in the ones place. Delete all the digits to its right.

4.82 rounded to the nearest tenth is 4.8.

✔ Quick Check
Round to the nearest tenth.

1 3.55

2 25.43

3 18.91

_____   _____   _____

Practice on Your Own
Round to the nearest tenth.

4 80.85

5 29.57

6 5.74

_____   _____   _____

7 31.43

8 7.18

9 12.48

_____   _____   _____

Identify Special Prisms

TEACHING STRATEGY

1. **Vocabulary** Help students understand prisms by discussing the terms *congruent* and *parallel*. If necessary, display two congruent parallel triangles and show how the triangles form the bases of a triangular prism.

2. **Teach** Review the Examples with students. Help students recognize key attributes of prisms. **Ask** What do all prisms have in common? [All of the faces are parallelograms and the two bases are parallel to each other.] What are some of the differences among them? [Possible answers: The shapes of their bases differ; they do not all have the same number of faces, edges, and vertices.] [8] Stress that the name for a prism is taken from the shape of its bases. **Ask** Why is the figure in Example 3 called a triangular prism? [The bases are triangles.] In fifth grade students learned that the top and bottom faces of a rectangular prism or cube were called the bases. In sixth grade students will learn that any pair of parallel faces can be the bases. In a triangular prism, there is only one pair of parallel faces, the triangular bases. In a rectangular prism or cube, there are 3 pairs of parallel faces.

3. **Quick Check** Look for these common errors as students solve the Quick Check exercises.
   - Confusing the faces and bases of a prism.
   - Incorrectly visualizing the parts of a 3-dimensional figure from a picture.

4. **Next Steps** Assign the practice exercises to students who show understanding. For students who need more support, provide tutoring using the alternate teaching strategy.

Additional Teaching Resource

🖱 Online Transition Guide with Reteach and Extra Practice worksheets from previous grade levels

ALTERNATE INTERVENTION STRATEGY

Materials: straws, string, tape, red and yellow construction paper

Strategy: Use a model to help identify special prisms.

1. Have students construct rectangular prisms. Using the straws as edges, students should thread the string through the straws and knot them to hold the straws together at each corner.

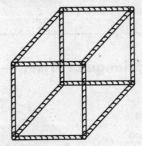

2. Have students examine their models. **Ask** How many straws did you use to build your prism? [12] Explain that the number of straws represents the number of edges in the prism. **Ask** How many knots did you tie to hold the straws together? [8] Point out that the number of knots represents the number of vertices in the prism.

3. Distribute construction paper. Have students tape the yellow paper to the faces and the red paper to the bases. **Ask** How many pieces of yellow paper are on your prism? [4] Explain that the yellow papers are the faces of the prism. **Ask** How many pieces of red paper are on your prism? [2] Explain that the red papers are the bases of the prism.

4. Have students trace the bottom base of the prism. **Ask** What is the shape of the prism's base? [a rectangle] Explain that this prism is called a rectangular prism because the base is in the shape of a rectangle.

5. Have students repeat the process to make a triangular prism.

Name _____

Date _____

Identify Special Prisms

A prism is a solid with two parallel, congruent bases that are joined by parallelograms called faces. The number of vertices and edges in a prism depends on the shape of its bases. A prism is named for the shape of its bases.

Example 1 **Cube**

The bases of a cube are squares.

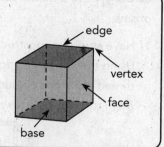

edge
vertex
face
base

Example 2 **Rectangular Prism**

The bases of a rectangular prism are rectangles.

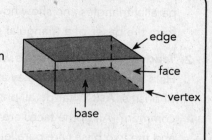

edge
face
vertex
base

Example 3 **Triangular Prism**

The bases of a triangular prism are triangles.

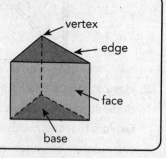

vertex
edge
face
base

✓ Quick Check
Name each prism.

1

2

3

_____   _____   _____

Practice on Your Own
For each prism, identify one base, one face, one edge, and one vertex.

4

5

6

_____   _____   _____

Find Areas of Rectangles, Triangles, and Trapezoids

G
SKILL 49

TEACHING STRATEGY

1. **Vocabulary** Make sure students understand the term *area*. **Ask** What is the difference between perimeter and area? [Perimeter is the measure of the distance around the outside of a figure, while area is the amount of space in the inside of the figure.]

2. **Teach** Review the examples with students beginning with Example 1. **Ask** In the formula $A = \ell w$, what does each variable stand for? [A is the area, ℓ is the measure of the length, and w is the measure of the width.] Focus on how each variable is replaced by the value for that variable. Refer to Example 2. **Ask** In the formula $A = \frac{1}{2}bh$, what does each variable stand for? [A is the area, b is the base, and h is the height.] What operation is indicated by bh? [multiplication] It is essential that students realize that the height must be perpendicular to the side used as the base in a triangle. Refer to Example 3. **Ask** In the formula $A = \frac{1}{2}(b_1 + b_2)$, what does each variable stand for? [A is the area, b_1 is one base, b_2 is the other base, and h is the height.] Point out that when calculating the area of either a triangle or a trapezoid, students must multiply by one-half.

3. **Quick Check** Look for these common errors as students solve the Quick Check exercises.
   - Neglecting to express the area as square units.
   - Forgetting to multiply by $\frac{1}{2}$ when calculating the area of a triangle or trapezoid.

4. **Next Steps** Assign the practice exercises to students who show understanding. For students who need more support, provide tutoring using the alternate teaching strategy.

Additional Teaching Resource
Online Transition Guide with Reteach and Extra Practice worksheets from previous grade levels

ALTERNATE INTERVENTION STRATEGY

Materials: TRT12 (Graph Paper)

Strategy: Use models to determine the areas of figures.

1. Distribute graph paper to students. Have them draw a rectangle that is 5 units long and 4 units wide.

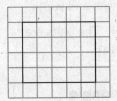

2. Have students examine their rectangles. Explain that area is the measure of the number of square units a figure covers. **Ask** How many squares are inside the rectangle? [20] How could you find the answer without counting the squares? [Multiply the rectangle's length, 5, by its width, 4.] What is the area of the rectangle? [20 square units]

3. Have students draw other rectangles with different dimensions and count the number of squares inside. Have them verify the area of each rectangle they draw by multiplying the dimensions. Be consistent in requiring students to give the area in square units.

4. Extend the lesson to triangles. Have students draw a rectangle that is 3 units by 6 units. Then have them divide the rectangle in half by drawing a diagonal line through opposite vertices of the rectangle.

5. Point out that the rectangle has been divided into two triangles that are the same size. **Ask** How many squares are inside the rectangle? [18] What part of the rectangle is each triangle formed by the diagonal? [one half] What is the area of each triangle? [9 square units] Draw students' attention to the fact that each triangle is half of the rectangle. You can divide the area of the rectangle by $\frac{1}{2}$ to find the area of one of the triangles.

Find Areas of Rectangles, Triangles and Trapezoids

Example 1 Rectangle

Find the area of the rectangle.

5 ft

7 ft

STEP 1 Use the formula for an area of a rectangle.

$A = \ell w$

STEP 2 Substitute the values for the length and width.

$A = 7 \cdot 5$

STEP 3 Multiply. The units are ft · ft = ft².

$A = 35 \text{ ft}^2$

Example 2 Triangle

Find the area of the triangle.

6 m

8 m

STEP 1 Use the formula for the area of a triangle.

$A = \frac{1}{2} bh$

STEP 2 Substitute the values for the base and height.

$A = \frac{1}{2} (8)(6)$

STEP 3 Multiply. The units are m · m = m².

$A = 24 \text{ ft}^2$

Example 3 Trapezoid

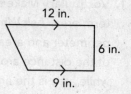

Find the area of the trapezoid.

12 in.

6 in.

9 in.

STEP 1 Use the formula for the area of a trapezoid.

$A = \frac{1}{2} (b_1 + b_2)h$

STEP 2 Substitute values for the bases and height.

$A = \frac{1}{2} (12 + 9)6$

STEP 3 Simplify. The units are in. · in. = in.²

$A = 63 \text{ in.}^2$

✓ Quick Check

Find the area of each figure.

1

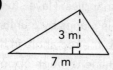

3 m

7 m

2

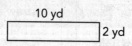

10 yd

2 yd

3

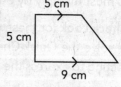

5 cm

5 cm

9 cm

_____   _____   _____

Practice on Your Own

Find the area of each figure.

4

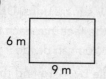

6 m

9 m

5

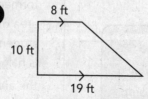

8 ft

10 ft

19 ft

6

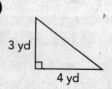

3 yd

4 yd

_____   _____   _____

Find Volumes of Rectangular Prisms

<table>
<tr><td>

TEACHING STRATEGY

1. **Vocabulary** Review with students the definition of *volume*. Discuss the following examples: the amount of water needed to completely fill a rectangular swimming pool and the amount of sand needed to fill a sandbox. Have students provide other examples of volume in their lives.

2. **Teach** Review the Examples and the formula for finding the volume of a rectangular prism with students. **Ask** In the formula $A = \ell wh$, what does each variable stand for? [A is the area, ℓ is the measure of the length, w is the measure of the width, and h is the measure of the height.] How is the formula for volume similar to the formula for area? [Possible answer: Both involve multiplying a figure's length and width.] How are they different? [Possible answer: For area, you only multiply two dimensions: length and width. For volume, you multiply three dimensions: length, width, and height.] Emphasize that units of volume are always cubic units, since volume is calculated by multiplying three dimensions. Refer to Example 2. **Ask** Since a cube has edges that are all the same length, what other method could you use to calculate the volume of a cube? [Possible answer: Find the cube of one edge.]

3. **Quick Check** Look for these common errors as students solve the Quick Check exercises.
   - Confusing the formulas for area and volume, and only multiplying the length and width of a rectangular prism to calculate volume.
   - Forgetting to cube the units of measure.

4. **Next Steps** Assign the practice exercises to students who show understanding. For students who need more support, provide tutoring using the alternate teaching strategy.

</td><td>

ALTERNATE INTERVENTION STRATEGY

Materials: connecting cubes or unit cubes

Strategy: Use models to find the volume of rectangular prisms.

1. Show students a connecting or unit cube. Explain that each cube represents one cubic unit of volume, each with length 1 unit, width 1 unit, and height 1 unit.

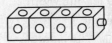

2. Connect 4 cubes horizontally. **Ask** What are the dimensions of the prism created by connecting the four cubes? [4 by 1 by 1] How many unit cubes are there? [4]

3. Review how to use the formula for volume ($V = \ell wh$). **Ask** If you use the formula, how many cubic units are there? [$4 \cdot 1 \cdot 1 = 4$ cubic units]

4. Next, connect four sets of three cubes horizontally. **Ask** How many unit cubes are there in all? [12] Connect two of the sets so they are side by side, and place the other two sets directly on top of them. This should form a 3 by 2 by 2 rectangular prism. **Ask** What are the dimensions of the prism? [3 by 2 by 2] How many cubes did you count? [12] Using the formula for volume, how many cubic units are there? [$3 \cdot 2 \cdot 2 = 12$ cubic units]

5. Have students work in pairs. Give each pair of students 20 cubes. Instruct them to build different sized rectangular prisms. Then have students find the volume of each prism by counting the cubes and by using the formula for volume. Students should build at least one prism that is a cube. [a 2 by 2 by 2 prism]

</td></tr>
</table>

Additional Teaching Resource

Online Transition Guide with Reteach and Extra Practice worksheets from previous grade levels

Find Volumes of Rectangular Prisms

Example 1 Rectangular Prism		**Example 2** Cube	

Example 1 Rectangular Prism

Find the volume of the prism.

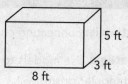
8 ft · 5 ft · 3 ft

STEP 1 Use the formula for the volume of a rectangular prism. $V = \ell wh$

STEP 2 Substitute the values for the length, width, and height. $V = 8 \cdot 3 \cdot 5$

STEP 3 Multiply. The units are ft · ft · ft = ft³. $V = 120 \text{ ft}^3$

Example 2 Cube

A cube is a special type of rectangular prism. The length, width, and height of a cube are all the same.

Find the volume of the cube.

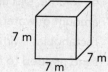
7 m · 7 m · 7 m

STEP 1 Use the formula for the volume of a rectangular prism. $V = \ell wh$

STEP 2 Substitute the values for the length, width, and height. $V = 7 \cdot 7 \cdot 7$

STEP 3 Multiply. The units are m · m · m = m³. $V = 343 \text{ m}^3$

✔ Quick Check

Find the volume of each prism.

1

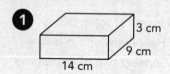
14 cm · 9 cm · 3 cm

_____

2

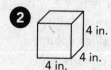
4 in. · 4 in. · 4 in.

_____

Practice on Your Own
Find the volume of each prism.

3

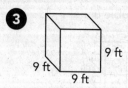
9 ft · 9 ft · 9 ft

_____

4

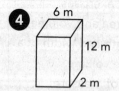
6 m · 12 m · 2 m

_____

5

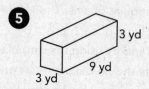
3 yd · 9 yd · 3 yd

_____

6

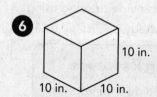
10 in. · 10 in. · 10 in.

_____

Interpret Data in a Line Plot

TEACHING STRATEGY

1. **Vocabulary** Make sure students understand the term *line plot* and can distinguish it from *line graph*.

2. **Teach** Explain that a line plot is used to visually display the frequency of the data. Point out that *frequency* refers to how often a data value occurs. Before reviewing the Examples, have students examine the line plot. **Ask** What does each x on the line plot represent? [one day of the week] Why are there 7 x's on the line plot? [There are 7 days in one week.] Review Example 1 with students. **Ask** What are you being asked to find? [The number of days last week on which 15 or more sandwiches were sold.] How do you find the answer using the line plot? [Count the number of x's on the line plot for 15 and 16.] Review Example 2 with students. **Ask** What are you being asked to find? [the least number of sandwiches sold in one day last week] How do you find the answer? [Look for the lowest value that has at least one x above it.] **Ask** What is the difference between the greatest number and least number of sandwiches sold each day? [5] How many sandwiches in all were sold last week? [96]

3. **Quick Check** Look for these common errors as students solve the Quick Check exercises.
   - Miscounting the x's on the line plot.
   - Confusing the frequency of the data with the data values themselves.

4. **Next Steps** Assign the practice exercises to students who show understanding. For students who need more support, provide tutoring using the alternate teaching strategy.

Additional Teaching Resource

🖱 Online Transition Guide with Reteach and Extra Practice worksheets from previous grade levels

ALTERNATE INTERVENTION STRATEGY

Materials: none

Strategy: Construct a simple line plot from data in a table. Then interpret the data.

1. Copy the following data table on the board.

Number of Books Read

Frank	2	Hannah	5
Marisol	4	Jeffrey	3
Jun	3	Simone	1
Keith	4	Rachel	4

2. Work with students to draw a line plot for the data. **Ask** What do the numbers below the line represent? [number of books read] What will each x on the line plot represent? [a student] How many x's should be placed above 5? [1] 4? [3] 3? [2] 2? [1] 1? [1]

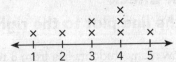

Number of Books Read

3. Have students interpret the data by asking them basic questions about the line plot. **Ask** How many students read 3 books? [2] What was the greatest number of books read? [5] What was the most frequent number of books read? [4] How many books were read in all? [26]

4. Discuss with students the differences between the data table and the line plot. **Ask** How does using the line plot make it easier to interpret the data? [Possible answer: The line plot displays the data in a visual way, so you can quickly and easily see the data.]

5. Repeat using another data set with numerical values. Begin with a frequency table and work with students to draw a line plot for the data. Then have students work in pairs to ask partners questions about the data.

Interpret Data in a Line Plot

Name _____ Date _____

Example 1

Mr. Kim recorded the number of sandwiches sold in his café last week. Each x represents one day.

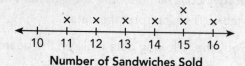

Number of Sandwiches Sold

How many days during the week did the café sell 15 or more sandwiches?

STEP 1 Examine the plot and count the number of x's for the values that are 15 or greater.

STEP 2 There are 2 x's for 15 and 1 x for 16.
2 + 1 = 3

15 or more sandwiches were sold 3 days last week.

Example 2

Look at the line plot for Example 1. What is the least number of sandwiches that the café sold during one day last week?

STEP 1 Examine the line plot and look for the least value that has an x above it.

STEP 2 11 is the least value on the line plot with an x above it.

The fewest number of sandwiches sold during any day last week is 11.

✔ Quick Check

Use the line plot to the right to answer the questions.

1 How many students live from 8 to 10 miles away from school?

_____

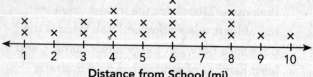

Distance from School (mi)

2 How many students live 5 miles or less from school? _____

Practice on Your Own
Use the line plot above to answer the questions.

3 Do more students live 3 miles or less from school or 7 miles or more from school?

_____

4 What percent of students lives 4 miles from school?

_____

5 What is the ratio of the number of students who live 8 miles from school to the number of students who live 2 miles from school?

_____

Divide Decimals by a Whole Number

TEACHING STRATEGY

1. **Vocabulary** Review with students the different terms related to division: *dividend, divisor,* and *quotient.* Write a division problem in both horizontal form and long division form. Have volunteers name each term in both forms.

2. **Teach** Explain to students that dividing decimals using long division is almost the same process as dividing whole numbers but that you must place the decimal point in the quotient before you begin to divide. Review the Example, emphasizing that it is absolutely necessary to place the decimal point in the quotient directly above the decimal point in the dividend. **Ask** Why do you start by dividing the ones and not the tens? [Possible answer: You cannot divide 3 tens by 4.] Why is regrouping necessary in Steps 3 and 5? [Possible answer: In Step 3, you cannot divide 1 ones into 4 equal groups. In Step 5, you cannot divide 2 tenths into 4 equal groups.] Make sure students understand that the quotient will not always have the same number of decimals places as the dividend. Point out that you cannot evenly divide 18 tenths by 4 in Step 3. This means the quotient will have digits that extend beyond the tenths place.

3. **Quick Check** Look for these common errors as students solve the Quick Check exercises.
   - Misplacing the decimal point in the quotient.
   - Incorrectly regrouping during the division process or forgetting to regroup.

4. **Next Steps** Assign the practice exercises to students who show understanding. For students who need more support, provide tutoring using the alternate teaching strategy.

Additional Teaching Resource

Online Transition Guide with Reteach and Extra Practice worksheets from previous grade levels

ALTERNATE INTERVENTION STRATEGY

Materials: place-value models

Strategy: Use place-value models to divide decimals by whole numbers.

1. Write 3.6 ÷ 3 on the board. Below the expression, draw a model to represent 3.6. Help students connect the model to the number by explaining that the models represents 3 wholes and 6 tenths.

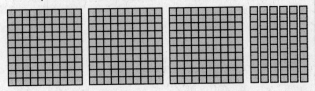

2. Work with students to separate the model into 3 equal groups. Each group will contain 1 whole and 2 tenths. **Ask** What is the quotient of 3.6 ÷ 3? [1.2]

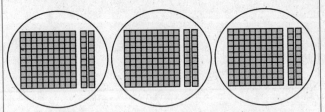

3. Repeat the exercise for 2.1 ÷ 2. Separate the 2 wholes into 2 equal groups of 1 whole each. Point out to students that you cannot separate the 1 tenth into two equal groups. Explain that you must regroup the 1 tenth as 10 hundredths. Revise the model to show the regrouping. **Ask** When you separate the 10 hundredths into 2 equal groups, how many hundredths are in each group? [5 hundredths are in each group.] What is the quotient of 2.1 ÷ 2? [1.05]

4. Once students are comfortable using the models to divide decimals by whole numbers, connect the models to the long division process. Write out each example above using long division, relating each step in the process to the steps you followed to separate the models into equal groups.

Divide Decimals by a Whole Number

Example

Divide 33.8 by 4.

STEP 1 Rewrite the problems for long division. Place a decimal point in the quotient directly above the decimal point in the dividend.

$$4 \overline{)33.8}$$

STEP 2 Divide the numbers as you would divide whole numbers.

33 ones ÷ 4 = 8 ones R 1 ones

$$\begin{array}{r} 8. \\ 4\overline{)33.8} \\ -32 \\ \hline 1 \end{array}$$

STEP 3 Regroup the remainder 1 one as 10 tenths and add the 8 tenths.

$$\begin{array}{r} 8. \\ 4\overline{)33.8} \\ -32 \\ \hline 18 \end{array}$$

STEP 4 Divide the tenths.

18 tenths ÷ 4 =
4 tenths R 2 tenths

$$\begin{array}{r} 8.4 \\ 4\overline{)33.8} \\ -32 \\ \hline 18 \\ -16 \\ \hline 2 \end{array}$$

STEP 5 Regroup the remainder 2 tenths as 20 hundredths.

$$\begin{array}{r} 8.4 \\ 4\overline{)33.8} \\ -32 \\ \hline 18 \\ -16 \\ \hline 20 \end{array}$$

STEP 6 Divide the hundredths.

20 hundredths ÷ 4
= 5 hundredths

$$\begin{array}{r} 8.45 \\ 4\overline{)33.8} \\ -32 \\ \hline 18 \\ -16 \\ \hline 20 \\ -20 \\ \hline 0 \end{array}$$

So, 33.8 ÷ 4 = 8.45

✓ Quick Check
Divide.

1 24.5 ÷ 2

2 14.08 ÷ 4

3 48.6 ÷ 3

Practice on Your Own
Divide.

4 15.06 ÷ 2

5 14.3 ÷ 10

6 47.7 ÷ 5

Find the Average of a Data Set

TEACHING STRATEGY

1. **Vocabulary** Review the term *average* with students. Note that some students may be more familiar with the term *mean*. Explain that both terms refer to the same measure of central tendency.

2. **Teach** Make sure students understand that you can only find the average of a set of quantitative data. **Ask** Can you find the average of data such as a favorite kind of car, favorite color, or favorite type of pet? Why or why not? [Possible answer: No; there are no numerical values.] Review the example with students. **Ask** How do you calculate the average of a data set? [Possible answer: Find the sum of the numbers in the data set and then divide the sum by the number of items in the data set.] Emphasize to students that when there is a 0 in the data set, it must be counted as one of the items in the set. Point out that the average of a set of whole numbers is not always a whole number. **Ask** Why is the average a decimal number? [Possible response: When dividing 453 by 5, you cannot divide the 3 ones by 5.]

3. **Quick Check** Look for these common errors as students solve the Quick Check exercises.
   - Forgetting to count 0 as part of the data set when counting the number of items.
   - Incorrectly calculating the sum of the numbers or the quotient for the average.

4. **Next Steps** Assign the practice exercises to students who show understanding. For students who need more support, provide tutoring using the alternate teaching strategy.

Additional Teaching Resource
🖰 Online Transition Guide with Reteach and Extra Practice worksheets from previous grade levels

ALTERNATE INTERVENTION STRATEGY

Materials: counters

Strategy: Use counters to find the average of a data set.

1. Write the following data set on the board: 2, 6, 4, 5, 3. Tell students they are going to find the average of this data set.

2. Distribute the counters to students. Have them put down the appropriate number of counters for each value in the data set.

3. Instruct students to combine their counters into one group. There should be 20 counters in all.

4. Have students look at the data set you wrote on the board. **Ask** How many items are in the data set? [5]

5. Tell students they need to separate the 20 counters into 5 equal groups. **Ask** How many counters are in each group? [4] Explain to students that this is the average of the data set. The average is the total value of the 5 items in the set divided evenly among the 5 items.

6. Repeat the exercise with the following data set: 2, 5, 4, 3. **Ask** How many counters are there in all? [14] How many items are in the data set? [4] Can you separate 14 counters into 4 equal groups? Explain. [No; there are 3 counters in each group with 2 counters left over.] Tell students they can divide each of the 2 counters left over in half. The resulting 4 halves can be divided evenly among the 4 groups. **Ask** How many counters are in each group now? [3 and a half] Write the number in decimal form as 3.5 and tell students that this is the average of the data set.

7. As students become more comfortable with using the counters to find averages, connect the modeling to the formula for finding the average: sum of items ÷ number of items in set.

Find the Average of a Data Set

Example 1

Find the average of this data set: 80, 96, 85, 100, 92.

STEP 1 Find the sum of the numbers in the data set.

$$
\begin{array}{r}
80 \\
96 \\
85 \\
100 \\
+\ 92 \\
\hline
453
\end{array}
$$

STEP 2 Count the number of items in the data set.
There are 5 items.

80, 96, 85, 100, 92

STEP 3 Divide the sum of the numbers in the data set
by the number of items in the data set.

$453 \div 5 = 90.6$

The average of the data set is 90.6

☑ Quick Check

Find the average of each data set.

1 8, 5, 7, 9, 6 _____

2 98, 75, 100, 96, 83, 88 _____

3 46, 86, 79, 27, 13 _____

4 $85, $73, $80, $93, $82 _____

Practice on Your Own
Find the average of each data set.

5 89, 83, 85, 81, 87 _____

6 72, 49, 55, 16, 30, 31, 62 _____

7 50, 42, 48, 42 _____

8 $14, $21, $12, $16, $26 _____

9 28, 15, 27, 39, 16 _____

10 30, 30, 50, 70, 20, 40 _____

11 7, 0, 12, 5, 6, 4, 8 _____

12 16, 19, 13, 20, 4 _____

Answers

Skill 1

Quick Check

1. 1, 2, 3, 6
2. 1, 3, 9
3. 1, 2, 5, 10
4. 1, 2, 3, 6, 7, 14, 21, 42

Practice on Your Own

5. 1, 3, 13, 39
6. 1, 7, 11, 77
7. 1, 2, 3, 4, 6, 8, 12, 16, 24, 32, 48, 96
8. 1, 5, 7, 35
9. 1, 2, 4, 5, 10, 20, 25, 50, 100
10. 1, 2, 3, 4, 6, 8, 9, 12, 16, 18, 24, 36, 48, 72, 144

Skill 2

Quick Check

1. 3, 6, 9, 12, 15
2. 10, 20, 30, 40, 50
3. 16, 32, 48, 64, 80
4. 21, 42, 63, 84, 105

Practice on Your Own

5. 5, 10, 15, 20, 25
6. 11, 22, 33, 44, 55
7. 15, 30, 45, 60, 75
8. 19, 38, 57, 76, 95
9. 25, 50, 75, 100, 125
10. 32, 64, 96, 128, 160
11. 45, 90, 135, 180, 225
12. 100, 200, 300, 400, 500
13. 111, 222, 333, 444, 555
14. 150, 300, 450, 600, 750
15. 250, 500, 750, 1,000, 1,250
16. 300, 600, 900, 1,200, 1,500
17. 500, 1,000, 1,500, 2,000, 2,500
18. 801, 1,602, 2,403, 3,204, 4,005
19. 1,000, 2,000, 3,000, 4,000, 5,000

Skill 3

Quick Check

1. 17
2. 19
3. 2, 5
4. 23

Practice on Your Own

5. 7
6. 19, 43, 137
7. 13
8. 31, 83
9. 17, 37, 61
10. None

Skill 4

Quick Check

1. 0
2. 65
3. 91
4. 8

Practice on Your Own

5. 155
6. 28
7. 15
8. 106
9. 33
10. 4
11. 10
12. 226
13. 200

Skill 5

Quick Check

1.
2.
3.

Practice on Your Own

4.
5.
6.

Skill 6

Quick Check

1. <
2. <
3. >

Practice on Your Own

4. >
5. <
6. <
7. <
8. <
9. >

Skill 7

Quick Check

1. 5.61
2. 2.72
3. 6.06

Practice on Your Own

4. 2.8
5. 9.01
6. 2.19
7. 10.33
8. 3.31
9. 8.93
10. 1.22
11. 14.32
12. 2.65

Skill 8

Quick Check

1. $7\frac{1}{2}$
2. $8\frac{1}{2}$
3. $6\frac{4}{5}$

Practice on Your Own

4. $9\frac{2}{3}$ 5. $5\frac{2}{3}$ 6. $4\frac{1}{2}$

7. $7\frac{2}{7}$ 8. $4\frac{3}{5}$ 9. $5\frac{1}{3}$

10. $9\frac{1}{4}$ 11. $7\frac{1}{6}$ 12. $6\frac{1}{3}$

Skill 9

Quick Check

1. $\frac{5}{2}$ 2. $\frac{17}{3}$ 3. $\frac{25}{4}$

Practice on Your Own

4. $\frac{37}{9}$ 5. $\frac{59}{8}$ 6. $\frac{13}{7}$

7. $\frac{59}{6}$ 8. $\frac{20}{3}$ 9. $\frac{22}{9}$

10. $\frac{30}{7}$ 11. $\frac{33}{5}$ 12. $\frac{35}{4}$

Skill 10

Quick Check

1. $\frac{2}{5}$ 2. $\frac{1}{6}$ 3. $\frac{2}{21}$

Practice on Your Own

4. $\frac{1}{3}$ 5. $\frac{1}{28}$ 6. $\frac{3}{35}$

7. $\frac{1}{24}$ 8. $\frac{5}{8}$ 9. $\frac{1}{14}$

Skill 11

Quick Check

1. Poss. answer: $\frac{2}{4}$ and $\frac{3}{6}$

2. Poss. answer: $\frac{6}{9}$ and $\frac{12}{18}$

3. Poss. answer: $\frac{6}{16}$ and $\frac{30}{80}$

Practice on Your Own

4. Poss. answer: $\frac{2}{8}$ and $\frac{3}{12}$

5. Poss. answer: $\frac{16}{20}$ and $\frac{20}{25}$

6. Poss. answer: $\frac{4}{14}$ and $\frac{16}{56}$

7. Poss. answer: $\frac{24}{27}$ and $\frac{40}{45}$

8. Poss. answer: $\frac{15}{36}$ and $\frac{20}{48}$

9. Poss. answer: $\frac{6}{40}$ and $\frac{9}{60}$

Skill 12

Quick Check

1. $\frac{2}{18}$ and $\frac{1}{9}$

2. Poss. answer: $\frac{3}{6}$ and $\frac{2}{4}$

3. $\frac{6}{10}$ and $\frac{3}{5}$

Practice on Your Own

4. Poss. answer: $\frac{15}{21}$ and $\frac{10}{14}$

5. Poss. answer: $\frac{24}{36}$ and $\frac{2}{3}$

6. $\frac{9}{14}$ and $\frac{18}{28}$

7. $\frac{10}{14}$ and $\frac{5}{7}$

8. Poss. answer: $\frac{24}{44}$ and $\frac{6}{11}$

9. Poss. answer: $\frac{12}{78}$ and $\frac{8}{52}$

Skill 13

Quick Check

1. 8   2. 63   3. 35

Practice on Your Own

4. 60   5. 24   6. 81
7. 18   8. 15   9. 5
10. 156   11. 3   12. 11

Skill 14

Quick Check

1. $\frac{2}{7}$ 2. $\frac{2}{3}$ 3. $\frac{1}{4}$

4. $\frac{3}{10}$ 5. $\frac{3}{7}$ 6. $\frac{1}{3}$

Practice on Your Own

7. $\frac{4}{7}$ 8. $\frac{1}{5}$ 9. $\frac{5}{7}$

10. $\frac{8}{9}$ 11. $\frac{3}{4}$ 12. $\frac{1}{3}$

13. $\frac{5}{6}$ 14. $\frac{4}{9}$ 15. $\frac{5}{8}$

15. $\frac{1}{10}$ 17. $\frac{2}{9}$ 18. $\frac{3}{10}$

Skill 15

Quick Check

1. 32 oz   **2.** 10 mL   **3.** 2 yd

Practice on Your Own

4. 16 qt   **5.** 1.5 g   **6.** 96 in.
7. 200 g   **8.** 3 pt   **9.** 0.45 m
10. 320 ft   **11.** 5 lb   **12.** 5,500 m

Skill 16

Quick Check

1. $P = 21; Q = 35$ **2.** $P = 36; Q = 18$

Practice on Your Own

3. $P = 72; Q = 24$ **4.** $P = 65; Q = 91$

Skill 17

Quick Check

1. 2,989   **2.** 9,585   **3.** 89,056

Practice on Your Own

4. 4,246   **5.** 4,465   **6.** 187,374
7. 365,850   **8.** 474,368   **9.** 10,584
10. 240,681   **11.** 9,222   **12.** 150,602
13. 4,160   **14.** 24,605   **15.** 61,425

Skill 18

Quick Check

1. $1\frac{1}{5}$ **2.** 3   **3.** $5\frac{1}{4}$

Practice on Your Own

4. 6   **5.** $2\frac{2}{5}$ **6.** 6

7. $\frac{3}{5}$ **8.** $2\frac{1}{2}$ **9.** $\frac{5}{6}$

10. $\frac{2}{3}$ **11.** $7\frac{1}{2}$ **12.** 2

Skill 19

Quick Check

1. $16\frac{1}{4}$ **2.** 24   **3.** $12\frac{6}{7}$

Practice on Your Own

4. $13\frac{1}{2}$ **5.** $13\frac{1}{2}$ **6.** $6\frac{1}{3}$

7. 12   **8.** $8\frac{6}{7}$ **9.** $4\frac{1}{5}$

Skill 20

Quick Check

1. $\frac{1}{8}$ **2.** $18\frac{2}{3}$ **3.** $\frac{7}{24}$

Practice on Your Own

4. $\frac{3}{20}$ **5.** $6\frac{2}{3}$ **6.** 128

7. $25\frac{2}{3}$ **8.** $10\frac{4}{5}$ **9.** 15

Skill 21

Quick Check

1. 3   **2.** $\frac{7}{9}$ **3.** $2\frac{1}{10}$

Practice on Your Own

4. $1\frac{1}{3}$ **5.** $\frac{3}{4}$ **6.** $1\frac{1}{5}$

7. $1\frac{9}{11}$ **8.** $\frac{11}{15}$ **9.** $\frac{9}{10}$

Skill 22

Quick Check

1. 21 cm   **2.** 54 qt   **3.** 121 km

Practice on Your Own

4. 56 g   **5.** 64 ft   **6.** 24 L

Skill 23

Quick Check

1. 1 : 20
2. 125 : 1
3. Possible answer: 6 : 16, 9 : 24
4. Possible answer: 18 : 20, 27 : 30

Practice on Your Own

5. 1 : 50
6. 6 : 1
7. Possible answer: 10 : 8, 15 : 12
8. Possible answer: 22 : 24, 33 : 36

Skill 24

Quick Check

1. 50; 20   **2.** 20; 25   **3.** 50; 28

Practice on Your Own

4. 50; 56   **5.** 20, 75   **6.** 25; 40
7. 50; 30   **8.** 50; 100   **9.** 20; 90

Skill 25

Quick Check

1. $\frac{14}{25}$ 2. $\frac{17}{20}$ 3. $\frac{23}{50}$

Practice on Your Own

4. $\frac{1}{2}$ 5. $\frac{1}{4}$ 6. $\frac{18}{25}$

7. $\frac{2}{3}$ 8. $\frac{3}{5}$ 9. $\frac{4}{7}$

Skill 26

Quick Check

1. 0.80   2. 0.65   3. 0.36

Practice on Your Own

4. 0.07   5. 0.54   6. 0.50
7. 0.23   8. 0.06   9. 0.44

Skill 27

Quick Check

1. 32   2. $7\frac{1}{2}$ 3. 9

Practice on Your Own

4. $22\frac{1}{2}$ 5. 8   6. 18

7. $28\frac{1}{3}$ 8. $31\frac{1}{2}$ 9. $9\frac{3}{4}$

Skill 28

Quick Check

1.
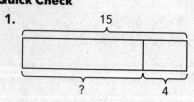

2.
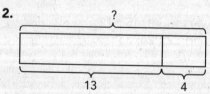

3.
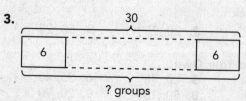

4.
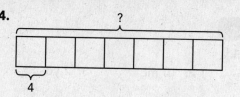

Practice on Your Own

5.
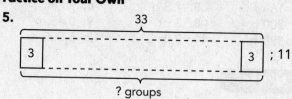
; 11

6.
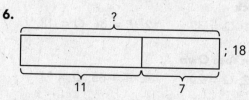
; 18

7.
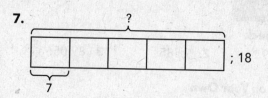
; 18

8.
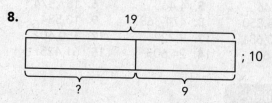
; 10

Skill 29

Quick Check

1. 1, 2, 3, and 6; 6   2. 1 and 2; 2
3. 1 and 3; 3   4. 2, 3, 4, 6 and 12; 12

Practice on Your Own

5. 1, 2, 3, 4, 6, and 12; 12
6. 1 and 5; 5
7. 1, 2, and 4; 4
8. 1, and 3; 3
9. 1, 2, 3, and 6; 6
10. 1; 1

Skill 30

Quick Check

1. product
2. quotient; dividend, divisor
3. difference
4. sum

Practice on Your Own

5. difference
6. sum
7. product
8. quotient; divisor, dividend

Skill 31

Quick Check

1. >
2. <
3. >
4. =

Practice on Your Own

5. <
6. >
7. =
8. >
9. <
10. <
11. >
12 =
13. >

Skill 32

Quick Check

1. $\dfrac{16}{y}$
2. 13s
3. $t - 5$
4. $34 + c$

Practice on Your Own

5. $7 - y$
6. $10 + x$
7. 56d
8. $\dfrac{m}{9}$

Skill 33

Quick Check

1. 17 and 23
2. 9 and 6
3. 14 and 2
4. 0 and 4

Practice on Your Own

5. 22 and 8
6. 18 and 66
7. 32 and 12
8. 7 and 35
8. 62 and 86

Skill 34

Quick Check

1–3

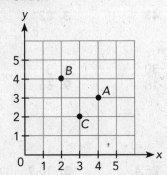

Practice on Your Own

4–10

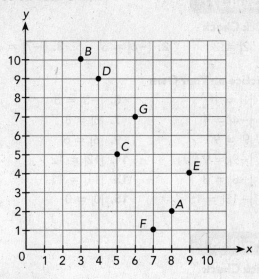

Skill 35

Quick Check

1. (2, 4)
2. (0, 6)
3. (3, 0)

Practice on Your Own

4. (1, 5)
5. (5, 1)
6. (0, 4)
8. and 9.

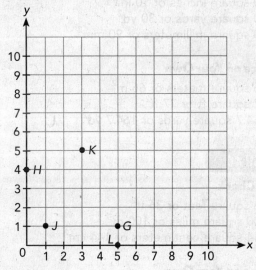

Skill 36

Quick Check

1. −5, −3, −2
2. −8, −4, −1
3. −10, −7, −5

Practice on Your Own

4. −11, −6, −3
5. −13, −11, −2
6. −10, −9, 2

Skill 37

Quick Check

1. $|2| = 2$ 2. $|-6| = 6$ 3. $|-7| = 7$

Practice on Your Own

4. $|1| = 1$ 5. $|-5| = 5$
6. $|-4| = 4$ 7. $|8| = 8$
8. $|9| = 9$ 9. $|6| = 6$
10. $|-9| = 9$ 11. $|12| = 12$
12. $|-8| = 8$ 13. $|11| = 11$
14. $|-15| = 15$ 15. $|0| = 0$

Skill 38

Quick Check

1. 9 in.   2. 30 ft   3. 25 m

Practice on Your Own

1. 16 cm   2. 22 ft   3. 31 mm

Skill 39

Quick Check

1. 10 square inches or 10 in.^{2}
2. 30 square yards or 30 yd^2
3. 90 square millimeters or 90 mm^2

Practice on Your Own

4. 66 square meters or 66 m^2
5. 77 square ft or 77 ft^2
6. 164.7 square yards or 164.7 yd^2

Skill 40

Quick Check

1. 36 square feet or 36 ft^2
2. 100 square miles or 100 mi^2
3. 144 square centimeters or 144 cm^2

Practice on Your Own

4. 625 square centimeters or 625 cm^2
5. 90.25 square inches or 90.25 in^2
6. 441 square millimeters or 441 mm^2
7. 213.16 square feet or 213.16 ft^2

Skill 41

Quick Check

1. trapezoid; $\overline{QT}$ and $\overline{RS}$

2. rhombus; $\overline{BE}$ and $\overline{CD}$, $\overline{BC}$ and $\overline{ED}$

3. parallelogram; $\overline{WZ}$ and $\overline{XY}$, $\overline{WX}$ and $\overline{ZY}$

Practice on Your Own

4. rhombus; $\overline{GJ}$ and $\overline{HI}$, $\overline{GH}$ and $\overline{JI}$

5. trapezoid; $\overline{SV}$ and $\overline{TU}$

6. parallelogram; $\overline{DG}$ and $\overline{EF}$, $\overline{DE}$ and $\overline{GF}$

Skill 42

Quick Check

1. 20.93   2. 47.317   3. 5.045

Practice on Your Own

4. 16.428   5. 15.6   6. 52.32
7. 19.018   8. 6.25   9. 25

Skill 43

Quick Check

1. 28.1   2. 8.2   3. 22.35

Practice on Your Own

4. 0.61   5. 14.03   6. 2.88
7. 4.57   8. 0.62   9. 12.48

Skill 44

Quick Check

1. 4.5   2. 38.07   3. 2.595

Practice on Your Own

4. 14.56   5. 21.50   6. 4.14
7. 0.084   8. 32.46   9. 27.93

Skill 45

Quick Check

1. 1.6   2. 2.03   3. 0.17

Practice on Your Own

4. 3.54   5. 0.72   6. 0.127
7. 2.5   8. 2.49   9. 0.088

Skill 46

Quick Check

1. 31   2. 43   3. 22

Practice on Your Own

4. 7   5. 30   6. 3
7. 31   8. 18   9. 66

Skill 47

Quick Check

1. 3.6   2. 25.4   3. 18.9

Practice on Your Own

4. 80.9   **5.** 29.6   **6.** 5.7
7. 31.4   **8.** 7.2   **9.** 12.5

Skill 48

Quick Check

1. triangular prism   **2.** rectangular prism
3. cube

Practice on Your Own

4. Bases: *ABC, DEF*: Faces: *ADEB, ADFC, BEFC*;
    Edges: *AB, AC, BC, AD, DF, FC, DE, BE, EF*;
    Vertices: *A−F*
5. Bases and Faces: *XWST, UVRP, PRST, RVWS,*
    UVWX, PUXT; Edges: *PR, RS, ST, PT, PU, RV, SW,*
    TX, UV, VW, WX, UX; vertices: *P−X*
6. Bases and Faces: *QPLM, NOKJ, JKLM, KOPL,*
    NOPQ, JNQM; Edges: *JK, KL, LM, JM, JN, KO,*
    LP, MQ, NO, OP, PQ, NQ; Vertices: *J−Q*

Skill 49

Quick Check

1. 10.5 m^2 **2.** 20 yd^2 **3.** 35 cm^2

Practice on Your Own

4. 54 m^2 **5.** 135 ft^2 **6.** 6 yd^2

Skill 50

Quick Check

1. 378 cm^3 **2.** 64 in.^{3}

Practice on Your Own

3. 729 ft^3 **4.** 144 m^3
5. 81 yd^3 **6.** 1,000 in.^{3}

Skill 51

Quick Check

1. 5   **2.** 10

Practice on Your Own

3. 7 miles or more   **4.** 15%
5. 3 : 1

Skill 52

Quick Check

1. 12.25   **2.** 3.52   **3.** 16.2

Practice on Your Own

4. 7.53   **5.** 1.43   **6.** 9.54

Skill 53

Quick Check

1. 7   **2.** 90
3. 50.2   **4.** $82.60

Practice on Your Own

5. 85   **6.** 45   **7.** 45.5
8. $17.80   **9.** 25   **10.** 40
11. 6   **12.** 14.4